✦ AT HOME WITH ✦
Gladys Knight

Gladys Knight with
Abe Ogden

 American Diabetes Association®

*Cure • Care • Commitment*SM

Director, Book Publishing, John Fedor; *Associate Director, Consumer Books,* Sherrye Landrum; *Editor,* Laurie Guffey; *Production Manager,* Peggy M. Rote; *Composition,* Circle Graphics, Inc.; *Cover Design,* The Magazine Group; *Nutrient Analysis,* Nutritional Computing Concepts, Inc.; *Printer,* Transcontinental Printing, Inc.

Printed in Canada
1 3 5 7 9 10 8 6 4 2

The suggestions and information contained in this publication are generally consistent with the *Clinical Practice Recommendations* and other policies of the American Diabetes Association, but they do not represent the policy or position of the Association or any of its boards or committees. Reasonable steps have been taken to ensure the accuracy of the information presented. However, the American Diabetes Association cannot ensure the safety or efficacy of any product or service described in this publication. Individuals are advised to consult a physician or other appropriate health care professional before undertaking any diet or exercise program or taking any medication referred to in this publication. Professionals must use and apply their own professional judgment, experience, and training and should not rely solely on the information contained in this publication before prescribing any diet, exercise, or medication. The American Diabetes Association—its officers, directors, employees, volunteers, and members—assumes no responsibility or liability for personal or other injury, loss, or damage that may result from the suggestions or information in this publication.

♾ The paper in this publication meets the requirements of the ANSI Standard Z39.48-1992 (permanence of paper).

Equal is a Reg. TM of Merisant Company. ©2001 Merisant Company.

ADA titles may be purchased for business or promotional use or for special sales. For information, please write to Lee Romano Sequeira, Special Sales & Promotions, at the address below.

American Diabetes Association
1701 North Beauregard Street
Alexandria, VA 22311

Library of Congress Cataloging-in-Publication Data

Knight, Gladys, 1944–
     At home with Gladys Knight / Gladys Knight with Abe Ogden.
         p. cm.
     Includes index.
     ISBN 1-58040-075-2 (pbk. : alk. paper)
     1. Diabetes–Diet therapy–Recipes. 2. Non-insulin-dependent diabetes–Popular works.
     I. Ogden, Abe, 1977- II. Title

RC662 .K587 2001
641.5′6314–dc21   2001041321

*To the memory of Elizabeth Knight,
my mother . . . and all people struggling
with diabetes.*

★ *Contents*

CHAPTER ONE

Meet Gladys Knight

★

When it comes to Las Vegas, almost everyone has an opinion. We've all seen it, whether it's being flashed across a movie screen, flickering its bright lights through our televisions, or monopolizing our senses as we actually walk down the streets of America's biggest adult playground. Everyone knows Las Vegas. We know the money, the showgirls, the mob bosses, the towering casinos, the cheap buffets—the list goes on. What most of us don't know, however, are the inconspicuous lives of generally conspicuous people who actually live in the infamous metropolis, making their home in the chaotic swirl of Nevada's money-soaked oasis.

Just a five-minute drive from the Luxor pyramid and the gray steel of Paris Casino's faux-tower lies the nondescript suburb of Henderson. In direct contrast to Vegas' glimmer and shine, Henderson's palm-lined avenues are filled with row upon row of modest, stucco-faced houses, grocery stores, and ubiquitous strip malls. Most of the homes are brand new, the lawns still revealing the cracked earth of the tan desert floor, and most have sensibly priced sedans parked in the bleached-white concrete driveways. Kids on bikes, skateboards, and just about anything else that rolls crowd the sidewalks and streets of the subdued cul-de-sacs. Everything seems ordinary and familiar, and if it wasn't for the omnipresent dry heat of the Nevada desert and the mountains peaking above the horizon, you could be anywhere in the United States. Which is why rolling into the driveway of a rock and roll legend, situated in this most unlikely of neighborhoods, can seem a little incongruous. Once you meet Gladys Knight, you realize that the inconsistencies between what you expect and what you get have just begun.

After passing through the gates at the entrance of her housing community (one of the few details that betray her music-legend status), you look for the big house—the four story behemoth with the Olympic-sized pool in the basement, the tennis court out back, and the line of Italian sports cars filling the eight-car garage. Instead, you find a modest, but impressive (it *is* Gladys Knight) home with three stories, a two-car garage, and a small, green lawn. You walk up to the large double doors and ring the doorbell. The door opens and there's Gladys with a bright, sincere smile that almost never leaves her lips. Her beautiful face beguiling her age, she invites you in.

In contrast to the pale façade of the stucco walls and clay tile of the roof, the interior of her house is bright with beautiful colors and tasteful arrangements. It would be easy to make the assumption that this is the work of a professional, but Gladys coyly admits that next to her family and music, interior decorating is one of her true loves. She spends hours sifting through tile samples, carpet books, and wallpaper designs and her enthusiasm pays off nicely. The spacious house is a beautifully realized accomplishment of pastels, earth tones, and floral patterns. Just like Gladys, her home is warm, down to earth, and inviting. Missing from the walls are the scores of gold records (they hang in the hallway of her mother's old home-turned-studio, La Mirada, just a few blocks away). Instead, the walls and cabinet tops are covered with pictures of her family members, all smiling and all just as beautiful as Gladys.

Like any gracious host, Gladys goes to great pains to make sure you're comfortable and enjoying your visit. She'll offer a welcome cold drink more than a couple of times (even in the dead of winter, the desert heat can produce a healthy thirst) and make sure you're in the most comfortable seat in the house. Unlike the self-absorbed divas we imagine music legends to be, Gladys is sincere in her desire to make you a welcome guest of her home. After a little bit of fussing, she finally sits herself, and with a hearty laugh that peppers most of her stories, she begins to relate the details of her life.

"I remember being a little girl and lying in bed fast asleep, and my dad would come home from his third job about midnight and quietly walk up the stairs into our bedroom. When he got into our room he would shine a flashlight in our eyes and wake us up and we'd hop right out of bed because we knew what he had in his hands. A big bag of Krispy Kreme doughnuts." It's a story Gladys likes to tell and she tells it with enthusiasm and her big, bright smile. How the story is received by others, however, depends on who is listening. Dietitians and physical trainers try their best not to pass out in horror. Doughnuts at midnight?! All those carbohydrates and fats just sitting in your stomach while you sleep! Others see it as another example of a time long gone, something that you'd never see in today's hectic hustle and bustle. But for Gladys, the story embodies all of the things that were important to her then and remain important to this day: family, consideration, and loved ones being brought together by a bond that unites like no other—food.

Of course, Gladys and her family aren't the only ones in America harboring a love affair with food. Americans are caught up in an escalating business of eating more and more food every day, raising the food industry to a multi-billion-dollar level. We like to eat, and unfortunately, what we like to eat the most are the wrong kinds of foods. Cheeseburgers, fried chicken, and pizza top most people's favorite foods list, while a majority of Americans get their vegetables in the form of the French fry. And as modern technology makes our lives more and more convenient, we aren't getting the exercise we need to keep this food from going straight to our bellies and hips. As a nation, we're getting pretty chubby.

Historically, African American cuisine hasn't been the healthiest food in the world—not a lot of tofu on the table around Thanksgiving time. But now, with a McDonalds on every corner, African Americans are beginning to make up a large majority of the fast food industry's best customers, with some pretty unsettling results.

The impact of the lifestyle change for this new "fast food generation" is not lost on Gladys—and not just because of its negative effect on people's health. More troubling to her is the sense of family and unity that is lost over a tray of burgers and fries or a pizza eaten in front of a television set. "Fast food has killed the art of conversation. When I was growing up, that's where we did most of our talking, over a meal. That's where I learned conversation, how to communicate. If people could just find at least one day a week to sit down and have a home-cooked meal, I think they'd be surprised at how close that can make them." And this is a philosophy Gladys practices just as diligently as she preaches. No matter how many perfor-mances, interviews, guest appearances, or engagements she has, she still tries to find at least one day a week to sit down together with her family and enjoy a big, home-cooked meal . . . a time when they can all be together, share their thoughts, and enjoy the art of conversation.

Fast food has killed the art of conversation.

An Alarming Situation

Of course, reviving the gift of gab between family members was not the only thing on Gladys' mind when she decided to share some of her favorite recipes and exercise tips with the

At a Greater Risk

You may not know it, but African Americans and other ethnic populations, such as American Indians and Latinos, are at a greater risk of developing diabetes. Researchers believe this may be because some ethnic groups have "thrifty genes" that helped them survive as hunters and gatherers when food was scarce. Now that food is plentiful and most people don't get enough exercise, these same genetic factors increase the risk of obesity, high blood pressure—and type 2 diabetes. This is especially true for black women. One study has shown that 15 percent of black women and 11 percent of black men have diabetes, as compared to 7 percent of white women and 7 per-cent of white men. Whatever the cause, the facts indicate that if you're African American, your chances of having diabetes are probably greater than you'd like.

world. Like those in the health care community, Gladys has noticed the astronomical rise in the number of cases of type 2 diabetes in the United States in recent years, especially in the African American community. As it stands, over 16 million people in the U.S. alone have diabetes, and of this number, 90 percent have type 2 diabetes. And this number is rising every day. Even teenagers—who are overweight and lacking in exercise—are developing type 2, which has traditionally been a disease of middle-aged or older adults.

But why? The answer is relatively simple—the majority of Americans do not live a healthy lifestyle. We eat too much, we eat the wrong foods, and we sit too much. Too many cheese-burgers and French fries are eating away at our health—filling our bodies with preservatives, hydrogenated fats, and choles-terol. Making the situation worse, the only exercise most Americans get is walking to the car.

Are You Overweight?

One way to determine whether you are over-weight is to compare your weight to this chart of acceptable weights for men and women.

Height Without Shoes (feet and inches)	Weight Without Clothes (pounds)	Height Without Shoes (feet and inches)	Weight Without Clothes (pounds)
4'10"	91–119	5'9"	129–169
4'11"	94–124	5'10"	132–174
5'0"	97–128	5'11"	136–179
5'1"	101–132	6'0"	140–184
5'2"	104–137	6'1"	144–189
5'3"	107–141	6'2"	148–195
5'4"	111–146	6'3"	152–200
5'5"	114–150	6'4"	156–205
5'6"	118–155	6'5"	160–211
5'7"	121–160	6'6"	164–216
5'8"	125–164		

Used with permission from the United States Department of Agriculture: *Report of the Dietary Guidelines Advisory Committee on the Dietary Guidelines for Americans*, 1995, p. 10.

This slow deterioration of health is not only something that Gladys has noticed, it's something that she has experienced firsthand. Like most families in this country, the Knight family has had its share of members struggling with unhealthy lifestyles and their consequences. Throughout her life, Gladys and many of her family members have battled with weight problems. In fact, Gladys checked into her first Weight Watchers program at the tender age of 16. That may sound like an early start, but this is the same early go-getter who started performing at the age of 8, helped form the Pips at 12, and was married and pregnant the same year she hit that Weight Watchers program.

But being overweight wasn't the only thing Gladys and her family had to contend with—diabetes made an appearance early on, too.

Just a Touch of the Sugar

When Elizabeth Knight, Gladys' mother, was diagnosed with type 2 diabetes at the age of 30, the condition was treated quite a bit differently than it is today. The insulin used to treat type 1 and advanced type 2 was still being extracted from animal sources, eating sugar was absolutely forbidden, glucose testing was a messy and inaccurate urine test, and the overriding message was pretty grim: if you had early-onset diabetes, you probably weren't going to live past 50. Still, many people with type 2 were surprisingly indifferent to their condition. The symptoms were subtle—a little thirst, a few more trips to the bathroom, some fatigue—and complications were a long way down the road. For most, type 2 just meant a little "touch of sugar."

For Elizabeth Knight, diabetes wasn't so easily dismissed. As a health care worker herself, Elizabeth Knight realized that diabetes wasn't something she could neglect. She also knew that discipline and knowledge were the best weapons against the disease.

Gladys recalls her mother's dedication with a sense of reverence and admiration. "There were lots of times that my mother would go to the doctor and know more about diabetes than her doctor. She felt that the more you know about something, the less control it has over you. And that's how she treated diabetes. She wanted to know as much about it as she could so the disease, and her doctors, had less control over her life. That's also why she made sure we knew as much about the disease as we could."

My mother . . . felt that the more you know about something, the less control it has over you.

What Is Diabetes?

Trying to sum up diabetes in a box is like trying to cook a casserole with one ingredient—there's a lot missing. To learn more about diabetes, check with the American Diabetes Association (call 1-800-DIABETES). For now, here are the basics.

Diabetes boils down to one thing—elevated blood glucose, or sugar. When there's too much glucose in your bloodstream, you have diabetes. But how do you get elevated blood sugar? It goes like this: The food you eat is all broken down into glucose or sugar. This isn't the same kind of sugar as table sugar, it's glucose. The cells in your body need glucose to operate; it's like the fuel for your cellular engine. To get the fuel into your cells, your body releases the hormone insulin to open the doors into your cells. However, some people don't produce insulin (type 1 diabetes) or the insulin in their body doesn't do a good job of opening the cell door to let the glucose in (type 2 diabetes). Researchers have a pretty good understanding of what causes type 1—the body destroys the area of the pancreas that produces insulin (though nobody knows why) and the person must have artificial insulin to survive. The causes of type 2, however, are not so clear. We do know that obesity, lack of exercise, race, and genetics play a big part. For some reason, these factors can interfere with how your body uses insulin, which means the glucose or sugar that was supposed to go in your cells slowly builds up in your bloodstream. After awhile, you have type 2 diabetes.

This education, however, didn't take place immediately. In fact, Gladys and her brothers and sisters didn't realize how serious her mother's diabetes was until Elizabeth started having complications about 20 years later. "My mother wasn't an alarmist. When she found out she had diabetes, she didn't run home and tell all of us. I learned about it in passing, hearing her talk to someone else about it. So we didn't think it was that serious. We just thought Mom was on a special diet."

Despite keeping her "special diet" low key, Elizabeth approached her condition the same way she approached any obstacle in her life: she just did it. Whatever changes her lifestyle called for, from caring for child stars to marriage difficulties to managing diabetes, Elizabeth forged ahead and accepted her responsibilities without complaining or self-pity. Well, most of the time, anyway.

"My mother was still human. She was strong-willed and dedicated, and she kept our family together the best she could. But she still had her moments when she got frustrated and just wanted to eat what she wanted to eat. This would last for a few days, and then she'd realize that she wasn't going to get anywhere acting this way. So after a little burnout, she'd always go back to treating herself right."

Her mother's determination and dedication is something that stays with Gladys to this day, though it took quite awhile for it to sink in. As a child prodigy, Gladys had a gift. It came easy to her and she never understood why that wasn't enough. Gladys will tell you straight up, "I hated to practice. I never understood the point." But that kind of attitude wasn't going to fly with Elizabeth. She made sure that Gladys always got the practice she needed, not so Gladys could reap the fame and fortune that her talent could afford her, but so she could develop her talent and realize the gift she had been given.

"My mom wasn't a stage mom. She didn't push us to be something that we weren't so her little kids could become stars. She had a knack for realizing what each of us could do and how to get us to use our gifts the best we could. Not in an overbearing way, just by helping us reach the best of our abilities."

This ability to push others towards realizing their greatest potential didn't stop with her children. As Gladys and her

Gladys (third from left) and Elizabeth (fourth from right) with the rest of the family.

brothers and sisters brought their own children into the world, Elizabeth provided the same guiding hand and encouraging attitude to her grandchildren. Ask anyone in the Knight family and they'll tell you—when it came to family, Elizabeth ran the show. She was the force behind the Knights, and she did it with grace, dedication, and genuine enjoyment.

But running a family is hard business, and it requires the utmost concentration and a lot of elbow grease. It's even harder when you have diabetes. Which is why Elizabeth made sure she maintained a healthy lifestyle and kept her diabetes in control. She wanted to take care of herself so she could take care of the ones she loved. She kept her diabetes in control for 50 years, keeping herself educated about the latest care techniques, maintaining her meal plan, and getting the exercise she needed. In the end, she gave all she could to her family and the world and passed away in 1998, leaving a legacy of love and caring, and a shining example to guide her family.

Spreading the Message

Of all the lessons her mother imparted to Gladys, one has always remained more important than the others—practice what you preach. In 1998, the same year her mother passed away, Gladys and the American Diabetes Association founded the Elizabeth Knight Fund, a special program designed to reach out to people with diabetes, their families, and other people at risk of developing diabetes. Gladys has devoted countless hours to helping others live better, fuller, and healthier lives. And because she realizes that she and her family are at a greater risk for developing diabetes (see the box below), she has worked to get herself and them into better shape, as well. But most importantly, she lives the same lifestyle she wants others to try.

Hand-Me-Down Genes

Your father's eyes or your mother's unfortunately full thighs may not have been the only thing you inherited from your parents and their parents before them. If someone in your family has diabetes, either type 1 or type 2, there's a greater chance that you can develop the disease as well. But don't worry, just because it runs in the family doesn't mean that you're destined to get blood sugar woes. It just means that living a healthy lifestyle is even more important for you. By keeping your weight under control and getting plenty of exercise, you drastically reduce your chances of developing type 2 diabetes, not to mention Mom's problem thighs.

Even though she doesn't have diabetes, Gladys soon realized that living a lifestyle aimed towards preventing diabetes was actually the healthiest way to live. In fact, the prescription for controlling and *preventing* type 2 diabetes is good for everyone—eat right and get some exercise. Living healthy is the best way to protect yourself against the threat of America's fastest growing "lifestyle disease," and it's the best way to get your body in tip-top shape. Gladys is a testament to that. There's a reason she looks as good as she does today. It's not surgery, and it's definitely not genetics, as you'll soon see—it's living a lifestyle designed to protect her from the same fate as her mother. She's dedicated to it and it's a lifestyle any person in the world can follow and enjoy.

CHAPTER TWO

Paving the Way

"Not being able to cook in my house just wasn't accepted. If you couldn't cook, you were like some kind of floozy." It may seem a little extreme, but growing up in Atlanta in the middle of the century, cooking wasn't just a skill, it was a birthright. The Knight family was definitely no exception. With recipes passed down from generation to generation like sacred heirlooms and every family get-together a celebration of southern cooking, making an appetizing meal was pretty important business. And Gladys picked up on this at an early age.

She may have been belting out Gospel Hymns at the age of three, winning national competitions at the age of eight, and rounding the Chitlin' Circuit in her early teens, but as a kid, Gladys took her cooking a lot more seriously than her singing. When her parents' friends would fuss over her big voice and tell her what a gift she had, she was thinking about heading into the back yard to make some mud pies. In fact, it was one of these mud pie cook-offs that planted in her a deep-rooted sense of the magic of cooking.

"My cousin Janice and I were in the backyard in Atlanta and had ourselves a pretend cooking party. We set up a table near a brook and put out a play tea set and got to pretending we were cooking twigs as carrots and mud as potatoes. Once we had everything all laid out on the table and our "bread" in the oven, we decided to go get our dolls to join us. When we came back about a half-hour later, we found the table steaming with a huge meal of real cooked carrots, potato cakes, and bread.

We were amazed. While my aunt watched from the kitchen window, we sat right down at that magical meal, and I have no doubt that experience is one of the reasons I've always gotten as much a kick out of cooking as singing."

From that moment on, Gladys spent as much time as she could in the kitchen with her mother and aunts and family friends. In that culinary-rich environment, the Knights set to work on producing some of the best food south of the Mason-Dixon line. Every Sunday mouth-watering fried chicken, Aunt Velma's famous corn off the cob with bacon and onions and peppers, spice cakes, and a host of other savory items appeared on the Knight family kitchen table. "Now, I'm not going to say that the Knight family of Atlanta, Georgia, *invented* soul food, but we definitely played a role in refining it to an art." Ask anyone who happened to sit down to one of those Sunday meals on a warm Atlanta day, and they'll agree whole-heartedly.

I've always gotten as much a kick out of cooking as singing.

A Rite of Passage

Gladys may have shown an early interest in the kitchen and the mysterious magic of preparing food, but her initiation into the Knight family of cooks required more than just a desire to join the team. Cooking good food and cooking it right was hard work, and Gladys had to prove that she was up to the task.

Any good cook will tell you that the ingredients make up about half of a successful recipe. The other half is a subtle mix of timing, intuition, and insider knowledge of some well-kept secrets. Some may add a pinch of salt in the most peculiar of places, while others might slide in a dash of soda for extra pop. But of all the family secrets handed down and followed like religious doctrine, probably none was as strenuous as the Knight family secret to the perfect cake.

"In my family, a cake mix had to be whipped 500 times before it was perfect. Not 499 and not 501—but 500 times. I remem-

A young Gladys takes a break from the rigors of touring.

ber the first time I tried to whip the cake mix. My mom asked me if I could do it and I told her of course I could, and I sat down and started whipping. I made it about halfway through and my arm felt like it was going to fall off. I tried and I tried to make it through, but I just couldn't do it. My sister had to finish the job. They say you get more than one set of hands in the cake and it will fall, and that one did and I was *so* disappointed.

"It took me a few times, but I finally got to where I could whip that cake mix 500 times and the first time I made it through was one of the biggest accomplishments of my life. It was like a rite of passage."

You ask Gladys about winning the *Ted Mack Original Amateur Hour* at the age of eight and she plays it off like just another thing she did as a little girl. Sure, being on the fifties equivalent of *Star Search* was exciting and new, and she met lots of wonderful people and had a great time. Sure, winning the award and becoming a hometown celebrity was fantastic, and the money was a nice bonus. All of these things were great, and Gladys recalls the memories with her cheerful laugh and omnipresent enthusiasm. But to her, these were just things that occurred because she happened to be born with an extraordinary voice. When she tells the story of that first time she made it 500 rounds with the cake, however, there's a certain richness and timbre to her voice that isn't there with recollections of other childhood milestones. There's a pride, a deep-rooted sense of accomplishment behind her words, and you realize that this event was something exceptional. This was one of her first steps towards becoming the woman she dreamed of being.

Growing Up and Growing Out

While cakes whipped 500 times may have been the road to personal and emotional growth for Gladys, it also paved the way for growth in less desirable areas. Fried chicken, fried pies, collard greens, and the rest of the soul food roster didn't help much either. Loaded in fats, calories, cholesterol, and gobs of other nutritional nightmares, these foods worked to add a few pounds here and there, making each Knight family get-together a little plumper than the one before.

Of course, when you're 5 years old, these loaded foods don't do a lot of damage (at least they didn't seem to then. See the box on the next page to find out how things have changed). Despite being a little national superstar, Gladys—with a lot of help from her family—lived a normal childhood lifestyle. She went to school every day, she had to make her bed in the morning, and she developed an ever-growing love of cooking. She bought her first cookbook at the age of 4 and cooked her first meal of scrambled eggs shortly thereafter. (The Gladys Knight secret to perfect eggs? Six drops of water—the fluffiest eggs you've ever seen!)

"I'm not going to say that [my] family invented soul food, but we definitely played a role in refining it to an art."

Gladys spent her afternoons cavorting around with her friends and family. Like most kids, climbing trees and playing tag until the sun went down usually kept the fat from sticking to Gladys' young bones. When you're on the go nonstop, your body does a good job of burning the fat and calories you'd otherwise store for later use.

As Gladys grew a little bit older, she stopped climbing trees and playing hopscotch with the neighborhood kids. She slowed things down and began to concentrate on her singing. After an impromptu backyard talent show she and her family

Little Billy Sure Is Growing!

In recent years, the incidence of childhood obesity has grown astronomically. Almost 30 percent of the children living in America today are obese. Like most things, there is no single cause for this expanding girth in grammar school tykes. Some people point to genetics and hormonal problems, but lack of exercise and a poor diet—at home and at school—is more than likely the culprit.

The growing number of obese children is alarming enough. However, an even more disquieting trend has emerged from this increasing weight problem—children with type 2 diabetes. A couple of decades ago, type 2 diabetes was considered a "mature-onset" disorder, thought to result from years of obesity and sedentary living. Children with type 2 were extremely rare. Now, doctors see children with type 2 diabetes more frequently than they'd like, and almost all of them are obese.

The best way to curb obesity in children is to help them develop a good eating plan, and even more importantly, make sure they get some exercise. By setting the foundation for healthy living now, you can pave the way for a healthy lifestyle down the road.

and friends threw together when she was just 8 years old, Gladys, her brothers, and two cousins decided to form a singing outfit and have a little fun. They didn't have a name then, but this motley group of characters would later become the initial incarnation of the Pips. Now, Gladys was belting R&B ballads instead of mud pies and climbing the social ladder at school instead of trees in the backyard. It may have been exciting, but this new lifestyle wasn't burning near as many calories. Unfortunately, her heavy diet of fried foods and baked treats hadn't changed.

Like others in her family, Gladys started to get a little plump as she entered into adolescence. Her family was tied together by rich, fatty soul food and this family bond was starting to show, and Gladys wasn't the only one to notice it.

"I remember my brother Bubba being so embarrassed for me, and himself, when I had to wear a leotard in front of the entire school for a modern dance performance. When we got home, the first thing he said was, 'Momma, please don't ever again let that girl be in something where she has to wear a leotard.'"

Gladys supervises as her nephew and her daughter, Kenya, imagine a life on the stage.

Gladys was 14 years old when she danced in front of the school in that unforgiving get-up. By this time, she had already won the *Ted Mack Original Amateur Hour*, was touring the nightclubs and bars of the southern Chitlin' Circuit with her brothers and cousins—now officially the Pips— and had an entire decade of performing under her belt. But despite being a seasoned veteran in front of the microphone before she could legally drive a car, Gladys was just starting her lifelong struggle with excess weight.

A Whole Lot of Chitlin'

About the time Gladys and the Pips were driving through the South and belting out performances to enthusiastic crowds, Gladys' mother, Elizabeth, received some disheartening news from her doctor. She had type 2 diabetes. This meant that the collard greens and fried pies were pretty much out of the picture. And what went for Elizabeth went for the rest of the family. Her special diet translated into a special diet for everyone, with a few exceptions aside. But just because the food Mom cooked was healthy fare didn't mean that the soul food of the past had disappeared from the Knight family meal plan.

Gladys will be the first to tell you that even though she was a paid performer, her life at home was as normal as ever. During the summers and on weekends she was singing pop songs in nightclubs and gospel hymns at church, but when school came back around in the fall, she was just another student. She concentrated on good grades, made the cheerleading squad, performed in the school jazz band, and worried about being in the "in" crowd, just like the rest of her peers. She also enjoyed big Sunday dinners and after-school snacks, which often worked against the healthy meals her mom tried to encourage. She also was emerging as a pretty terrific cook herself, whipping out family recipes to the delight of her friends, family, and weekend touring buddies. Suddenly, though, those leotard appearances were looking pretty bad.

At the tender age of 16, Gladys enrolled herself in her first Weight Watchers program (with many to follow in the future), and had little success. She showed some improvement, but it was short-lived and soon the weight was right back on. Of course, at 16, Gladys experienced one of the most eventful years of her life, and you can't really blame her for not sticking to her program. When most people are spending their first carefree years behind the wheel of a car or cheering through Friday night football games, Gladys was braving a long streak of trials and tribulations. This was also the first time she would encounter a conflict in lifestyles that would last the rest of her career.

Choosing a Path

In 1961, Gladys graduated from Archer High School in Atlanta, Georgia. That same year, she married her high school sweetheart, Jimmy, and got ready for a new addition to the family. Meanwhile, her career with the Pips was starting to really take off. Their songs were played on the radio (sometimes without the Pips' consent) and they were touring the country and wowing crowds from coast to coast. That's a lot to juggle at once, especially for someone in her mid-teens, and the pressure finally began to wear on Gladys with very negative effects. A few months into her first pregnancy, while on tour, she lost her baby. The loss was devastating to Gladys, and when she became pregnant soon after, she decided that raising a family took priority over touring with the group. The hustle and bustle of the performing lifestyle had already produced one tragedy and she figured that was enough. When her son, Jimmy, was born nine months later, Gladys decided that her performing days were done. She moved to Atlanta with her husband and devoted herself to being a mother. Her days were spent decorating the new apartment, with the family tradition of the big Sunday dinner gladly revived. And Gladys couldn't have been happier.

"I think I took more pleasure decorating our first little nest than I did from two weeks worth of singing. I had always dreamed of having a place of my own and taking care of it and my family . . . . It was one of the most peaceful times in my life."

But the days of peace didn't last long. Her husband was a struggling jazz musician and raising a family on a saxophone player's salary was pretty tight. Up in New York, the Pips were having a pretty good go without Gladys, but they were a long way from where they were when she was dancing and singing with them. Gladys knew that if she went back to the Pips, they could get back on track and she could make some money. To help her family, Gladys returned to her career, and went on to make rock and roll history.

A Little of Each

Just because Gladys was criss-crossing the country to perform with the Pips didn't mean that the homemaker she left behind was gone forever—just the contrary. Everywhere she went, Gladys brought that Knight family domestic touch with her. And more importantly, she always put her families first—both of them. Whether it was her mother, Jimmy, Kenya, Shanga, or anyone related by blood; or a member of her larger, rock and roll family, Gladys always made sure they were well taken care of. When others were drinking and partying, Gladys was backstage putting together some home cooking.

"I've long been known for my ability to whip up good home cooking on the road. Over the years I've cooked for everyone from Luther Vandross to Jamie Foxx to Tom Jones, from Stevie Wonder to B.B. King. One night, Sammy Davis Jr. went into a conniption because he came late for dinner and all of my black-eyed peas had been gobbled up."

I've long been known for my ability to whip up good home cooking on the road.

Of course, Gladys' ability to bring a little bit of home life with her on the road had its worrisome side, too. When the group was first starting out and roaming the Chitlin' Circuit of the south in a beat-up old car, they were lucky to get a hot dog for dinner. Needless to say, watching their weight wasn't a high priority on the foursome's list of things to do. But by the mid-sixties, things were starting to pan out pretty good for Gladys and the Pips and their next meal wasn't a big question mark. Pretty soon, Gladys' collard greens and fried chicken were starting to show again, and Gladys resumed her roller-coaster ride with weight.

Through the years, Gladys has been through more weight loss programs than she can count. She's been through gold records, Grammy awards, marriages, and the start of a solo career—so many extraordinary events that it seems overwhelming. But underneath the celebrity persona, Gladys is just a girl from Atlanta with a big voice and a love for family and friends. She's also just another person who's been through the ups and downs of dieting and exercise. Sometimes her plan would work; sometimes it wouldn't. More often than not, she'd find herself right back where she started. Until one day she received a gift that would change her life.

What a Gift

Gladys' problems with weight were not only her own. Unfortunately, a little extra skin ran in the family, and her youngest son, Shanga, experienced the same problem with weight that had plagued his mother. In fact, it had become so bad that he was having trouble doing the things he loved to do, like play basketball. He could barely make it from one end of the court to the other. His father noticed this, so he decided to get him some professional help. He also decided to extend the present to Gladys.

"Shanga's father called one day and said that he had a birthday gift for me on the way over to my house. I had no idea what it was. My doorbell rang and there my gift stood, a good-looking professional trainer named Al Claiborne."

And what a gift it was. With Al's help, Gladys (and Shanga) developed a plan for healthy living that finally worked. After all the years of dieting and weight programs that never seemed to last, Gladys had stumbled upon a recipe for living that got her the results she had been searching for—a recipe for living that she wants to share with the rest of the world.

CHAPTER THREE

Eating Right and Loving Life

When Al first met Gladys, he realized that they had a lot of work to do. It wasn't that Gladys had completely let herself go, she had just fallen into a lifestyle and a routine that were slowly eating away at her health. She had been through Weight Watchers and other diet programs, and they had worked for awhile. But they never helped her change her attitude about eating. Pretty soon, she would be right back where she started, sometimes even heavier than before. What Al wanted to do was create a different lifestyle and routine that would do more for her—take off weight, add muscle, and provide energy to be a better singer, mother, and grandmother.

Lifestyle Shock

With Al's help, Gladys came to realize that she was not going to lose weight and get a better figure with short-term thinking. To get to where she wanted to go, to be a healthy person, she had to live a healthy lifestyle every day. Al also knew that creating a habit of living that was good for both body and mind didn't come from making sudden, drastic changes to her daily routine. If things change too quickly, if you're suddenly living in a way that's completely alien to you, chances are you're not going to stick with it very long. Why? If it doesn't feel like your life anymore, you and your body will suffer a "lifestyle shock." The diet or exercise program becomes a chore, something you labor through. You'll stick with it just long enough to lose a few pounds, or fit into the outfit you've been dying to wear, and then you'll quit. Soon, you'll be right back to where you were before because it's comfortable and familiar. The key to healthy living is to make small changes, changes you can live with, until you can't imagine living any other way.

When Al met with Gladys, he saw that what she wanted to accomplish would be quite a project. Her long hours on the road and changing schedule at home would make regular exercise and balanced meals a challenge. But working together, they created a fitness plan that Gladys could live with, a way of living that she enjoys today. She looks forward to her morning workouts because now she's looking like she wants to look, feeling how she wants to feel, and enjoying a brighter, fuller life. It didn't require drastic changes, unbearable diets and starvation, or 4-hour workouts every day. It just took a little bit of tweaking to her everyday routine over a long period of time—the same tweaking you can do to get the results you want.

But What about Diabetes?

Sure, this all sounds great for people looking to lose a few pounds or look better. But, you may ask, what does all this have to do with diabetes? The answer is, everything. If you're

What's My Risk?

You are more likely to have type 2 diabetes if you

- Have relatives with diabetes
- Are overweight
- Are American Indian, Latino, or African American
- Are at least 45 years old
- Have impaired glucose tolerance (your body's insulin doesn't work as well as it should, so your blood sugar is too high)
- Have high blood pressure
- Have high blood fats
- Had gestational diabetes or delivered a baby weighing more than 9 pounds

suffering from type 2 diabetes, you're probably also suffering from what many doctors are now calling a "lifestyle syndrome." This means that your diabetes is, in large part, caused by the lifestyle that you're living. Most cases of type 2 diabetes result from a person being overweight and not getting nearly enough exercise. While genetics play a role in the process, sedentary living (too much sitting) is almost always the culprit. Gladys is already at risk for developing diabetes since her mother had the disease, but her old lifestyle made the risk much greater. And being African American also adds to her risk. By exercising regularly and eating better, Gladys is doing more than getting in shape—she is doing everything she can do to prevent diabetes from developing.

The good news is that changing your lifestyle is the best medicine for type 2 diabetes. This is how you treat it and how you can prevent it as well. In fact, if you change your pattern of living enough, you can actually reverse the advancement of diabetes and the negative effects it has on your body. With proper diet and some good old-fashioned daily exercise you won't need insulin and you may not even need diabetes pills. Talk to your doctor before doing anything to change your lifestyle, especially if you have never exercised before. But chances are, you'll find that a lifestyle plan, much like the one Gladys uses to look and feel great, will work wonders for you and your diabetes.

How to Care for Your Diabetes

While the management of diabetes can be both challenging and complex, the basic outline to healthy living is relatively simple.

- Eat healthy foods.
- Control your weight.
- Stay physically active.
- Take diabetes pills or insulin if you need them.
- Check your blood glucose.
- Get regular check-ups.

Just because you don't have diabetes right now doesn't mean that you're not at risk. This lifestyle syndrome can affect just about anybody. If you have family members with diabetes and you're not living the healthiest of lifestyles, you're at an even greater risk. By changing your lifestyle now, you're going to feel better and look better, AND you're going to drastically reduce your chances of developing one of the fastest-growing diseases in the nation.

Two-Pronged Attack

Every healthy lifestyle plan that's going to produce lasting results has a two-pronged attack—healthy eating and exercise. You can "diet" all you want, but if you're not getting any exercise, you're not going to see long-lasting results. Conversely, if you're getting lots of exercise and you're still eating chicken-fried steak for every meal, you're probably going to have some extra meat on your bones. The key is to find a healthy balance of food and exercise that not only keeps your body in tip-top shape, but makes you feel so good you don't run back to your old way of living. You have to make changes that you can live with.

So what's your first step? Cut down on the fatty foods and the calories and hit the treadmill a little more often? Too many changes. Just choose one—for example, focus on dropping a fatty food like doughnuts or fried chicken. Even then, we all know it's not that simple. Eating can be one of the most pleasurable pastimes in the world, and nothing tastes better than fats and sugars. Or, for that matter, your mom's fried chicken, mashed potatoes, and pecan pie. It's not easy to stop eating the foods you've grown up eating and to start choosing more vegetables and healthier ways of cooking them. You're entering strange, sometimes uncomfortable territory when you do, and it takes courage to keep going. To help you in your quest, the recipes in this book were developed by Al and Gladys to get you on your way to healthy eating. They're delicious, easy to make, and good for you, too.

Exercise is also a tough habit to get into. Living an easygoing, sedentary lifestyle tends to leave your body capable of only living a sedentary lifestyle. Muscles grow weak from disuse—

your heart muscle, especially—and your weight starts to climb. All of this makes even mild exercise uncomfortable, and you want to avoid it. You take the elevator instead of the stairs, you have the bag boy carry your groceries instead of carrying them yourself, you ride a mower to mow the lawn instead of pushing one, and so on. Of course, all of this is a sort of chicken-before-the-egg type of problem. Did being out of shape cause you to take the elevator, or did using the elevator and similar technologies keep you out of shape? The good thing about exercise is that after getting over the initial hurdle, the more exercise you get, the more you want. Exercise and getting in better condition makes you feel so good that you begin to crave it and fit more of it into your daily routine.

Neither One of Us

Wants to Say Goodbye to the Cheeseburger

You can't deny it—fatty foods taste good. Really good. As a nation, America consumes more fatty foods than any other nation on the planet. But where does America's love affair with the French fry come from? The answer is nature.

There's a reason your body loves fats and drives you to eat as much of them as possible. Thousands of years ago, before the drive-thru and the super-sized meal, humans weren't exactly sure where their next meal was coming from, or when it was going to come. Sometimes, it would be days before a substantial meal would come their way. So what helped them survive when food was few and far between? Fats. When your eating is erratic, fats are your body's best friends. They store away nicely (in the abdomen of men and the legs and hips of women) to be used for a hungry, rainy day. They were, and still are, an excellent source of energy used up more slowly than other forms of body fuel, such as carbohydrate. Which is why we harbored such strong cravings for fat, and continue to even now. Our body wants fats so it can survive until the next meal. In essence, fat is the body's survival pack.

That was great thousands of years ago when we didn't get much fat in our meals, eating mostly fruits, vegetables, nuts, and berries to tide us over until the next big animal kill. But now, when our next meal is rarely longer than four hours away, too much fat works against our bodies and eventually leads to some pretty nasty health conditions. Heart disease, stroke, and type 2 diabetes are just a few of the problems that can come with an expanding waistline. Even worse, many of the fats we take in are saturated fats from meats, cheese, and the infamous French fry. We also eat a lot of hydrogenated fats from highly processed foods such as store-bought cookies, breads, and margarine. Of all the fats, none are worse than trans fats, which also make an appearance in processed foods. You avoid these, and your health rating will rocket. Also keep in mind that there are good fats as well as bad fats. Most of these good fats come in liquid form, primarily in cooking oils like canola, sunflower, and olive oil.

Your body stores fat, and turns to carbohydrate (its favorite fuel) for energy before resorting to stored fat. This means that if you're eating a high-carb, high-fat diet, your body's going to use the carbohydrate before it uses the fat. Furthermore, your body will store unused carbohydrate as fat. This means that even if you eat no fat at all, but so much carbohydrate you don't burn it all, you're going to get more stored fat. Carbohydrates are healthy foods, but too much of a good thing is

Diabetes and Carbohydrate

Carbohydrates come in rice and potatoes, breads and cereals, and sweets like brownies and ice cream. You also find carbs in fruits, milk, and vegetables. Clearly, some carbs are better for you than others, but they all raise your blood sugar—which is why counting the grams of carbohydrate that you eat helps control your blood sugar better if you have diabetes.

You may not realize it, but all foods are broken down to glucose—a form of sugar—no matter what the food is. In essence, sugar is just another carbohydrate. A brownie and a baked potato have about the same effect on blood glucose, which is actually pretty good news for people with diabetes. The old "no sugar whatsoever" rule of the past no longer applies. Now you can enjoy foods with sugar just so long as you count them as a carbohydrate in your meal plan.

Gladys and The Pips getting ready to hit the stage at an award show in 1984.

A young Gladys and The Pips take a break from the Chitlin' Circuit for some ice cream.

Left: Gladys takes a curtsy after winning the *Ted Mack Original Amateur Hour* contest at the age of 8.

Below: Gladys and The Pips on stage for the *Summer Series Television Show* in 1975.

Gladys with her son, Shanga, at her *50 Years in Show Business* anniversary celebration in 1999.

Right: Gladys, Elizabeth Knight (third from left, top row), and family at Gladys' granddaughter's baptism in Las Vegas, 1993.

Left: Gladys with Bill and Hillary Clinton in the spring of 1997 after giving a live performance on PBS for the President and First Lady.

Above: Gladys with her children and grandchildren.

Below: Gladys and her daughter, Kenya, at the grand opening of Kenya's gourmet bakery in Las Vegas.

Gladys with her grandchildren.

Above: Gladys and crew at a Friends and Family Weekend in Las Vegas, fall 2000.

Gladys with her granddaughter at her granddaughter's second ballet performance in 1998.

not healthy, either. When you're eating carbohydrate, just be sure to watch your serving size. Carbohydrate poses some unique problems for people with diabetes (see the box on the previous page).

So what do you do? Do you cut out fats and carbohydrate and sugar and eat nothing but celery stalks and carrots for the rest of your life? Of course not. Gladys didn't do that to get where she is today. There's no way you could stick to that meal plan, and it would be unhealthy for your body. You need fats and carbohydrate to function properly. The key, as you'll soon see, is to eat many different foods but not too much of any one food. Focus on getting the right kinds of fats and carbohydrate—and most importantly, the right amount.

A Simple Rule

When Al walked into her life, despite the diet plans and the expensive diet programs, Gladys was a far cry from the healthy, fit person she is today. Living on the road with poor eating habits and not enough exercise was taking a toll, and Gladys was beginning to get fed up. "I was tired of shying away from the camera every time someone wanted to take my picture. I was tired of feeling uncomfortable in my clothes. I was tired of feeling self-conscious. By the time Al came into my life, I was ready for a big-time change."

Trouble was, Gladys didn't know how to approach her problem. She would go on the latest fad diet (which, we'll see later, can often wreak havoc on your body), lose a few pounds, and pretty soon, be right back where she started. The first thing Al recognized was that Gladys didn't know how to live in a way that was both good for her body and pleasant enough to stick with. So right off the bat, Al decided to lay down some ground rules to help Gladys on her way to better living. When it came to eating, Al had only one:

If you can't wash it, don't eat it!

A pretty simple rule, huh? If you can't clean it off, if it's not durable enough to stand a good washing, just don't eat it. But why? Does washing hold some mysterious power that allows food to magically develop nutrients? Does washing whisk away the fats and cholesterol? Not at all. It's something much more simple than that. However, to truly understand where Al's coming from, it helps to know a little more about his general philosophy towards fitness.

Keep It Natural

Al's a strong believer in the power of nature. The way he sees it, we all came from nature, and are still a part of nature (in spite of the cars and air conditioning and supermarkets). Thus, the best way to live our lives is in a way that's connected with nature. This is the reason for Al's simple rule to eating. If you can wash it off, then there's a good chance you're eating something fresh and close to the earth—not something that's highly processed and manufactured. The more recently your food came from the earth, the more vitamins and minerals and nutrition it has for you. If your food can sit in a box on the shelf for a year, how much can it do for you?

Some of the foods that stand up to the wash test include:

- Fruits
- Vegetables
- Most meats
- Seafood
- Rice, grains, and beans

The list of things you can't wash, however, goes on and on. Our markets are flooded with foods that are highly processed in boxes and bags and cans. They're as far from being natural as possible and all that processing removes vitamins, minerals, and fiber that your body needs. Can you wash a cheeseburger? Not unless you enjoy soggy sandwiches. So the wash test is a simple way to weed out less healthy, highly processed foods and make sure you eat foods that are good for you. But what's the point?

It's All Connected

It all goes back to Al's philosophy. Not only are we a part of nature, but we're also a self-contained organism that's completely interconnected. What we do to one part of our body has lots of effects on other parts of our body. This idea will come into play more when we discuss exercise, but it has an impact on how we eat, too.

As Al tried to impress upon Gladys, when we eat processed foods, we're taking in a lot of trans fats. If the food label lists hydrogenated vegetable oil, you're getting what may be the most unhealthy fats you can eat. They are man-made saturated fats, and our bodies are not really sure what to do with them. These fats can end up plastered against the walls of your blood vessels, causing your circulation to become impaired.

Unprocessed natural foods—not in boxes or bags—are what our bodies were designed to use. Nutrients from fresh and frozen fruits and vegetables, lean meats and seafood, and grains and beans keep us going in a healthy manner. Al sums it up nicely when he suggests, "Think of natural foods as high-octane fuel for the engine of our anatomy."

Natural foods [are] high-octane fuel for the engine of our anatomy.

Making It Right for You

Unfortunately, switching to a meal plan of all-natural foods can seem pretty overwhelming to a lot of people who aren't used to eating healthy. If, like Gladys, you're used to fried pies and collard greens, or even fast food, the thought of eating raw vegetables like asparagus every day can send shivers down your spine. And that's understandable. The thing to remember is that you don't want to make drastic changes right out of the gate. Ease into a new way of eating slowly, so your body goes into less of a "lifestyle shock."

When you're just starting out, try to include one or two healthy foods in with, or instead of, the foods you enjoy now. Then, try to phase out those fried foods that you've become accustomed to. If you fry foods every day, try another way of cooking, such as stir-frying or boiling, one day out of the week. Remember, make it something that you'll enjoy so that you don't give up. Make little changes that add up over time to healthier meals overall.

Take Gladys, for example. Instead of tossing out the foods she had lived with for so many years, Al just added a few tweaks to her regular meals. Instead of frying food, they'd try stir-frying with olive oil. Instead of red meat for a main course, they substituted chicken or seafood. And for snacks, he encouraged fresh fruits instead of fatty, packaged chocolates. This didn't happen all at once, either. These were changes that were eased in over a period of time, and now Gladys can't imagine eating any other way.

What's a Food Pyramid?

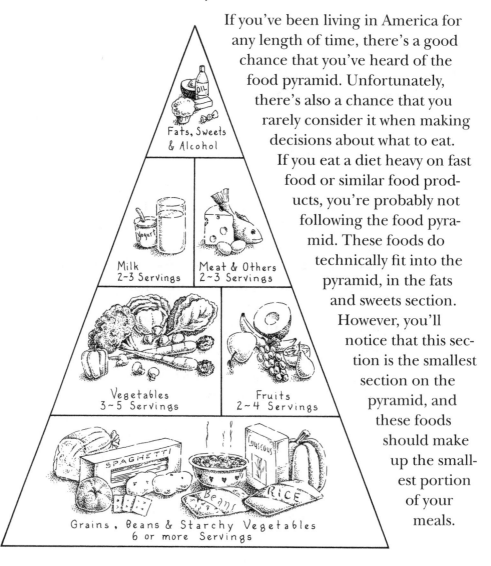

If you've been living in America for any length of time, there's a good chance that you've heard of the food pyramid. Unfortunately, there's also a chance that you rarely consider it when making decisions about what to eat. If you eat a diet heavy on fast food or similar food products, you're probably not following the food pyramid. These foods do technically fit into the pyramid, in the fats and sweets section. However, you'll notice that this section is the smallest section on the pyramid, and these foods should make up the smallest portion of your meals.

The fact is, the food pyramid is the easiest way to organize your meal plan. It may seem simple, but it's the foundation Gladys and Al use to create the meals they enjoy every day. And if you have diabetes or are trying your best to curb your chances of developing diabetes (as Gladys is), the food pyramid is a big help. Again, work in foods from the bottom of the pyramid one or two at a time, trying to avoid a complete meal plan overhaul right away. If you stick with this easy-to-follow guide, you'll get long-lasting results you won't get from other fad diets.

Dietary Recommendations

Interestingly enough, the Department of Health and Human Services and the U.S. Department of Agriculture (USDA) developed dietary guidelines for a healthy diet and lifestyle that fit right in with Al's simple rule.

- Aim for fitness.
  Aim for a healthy weight.
  Be physically active each day.

- Build a healthy base.
  Let the pyramid guide your food choices.
  Choose a variety of grains daily, especially whole grains.
  Choose a variety of fruits and vegetables daily.
  Keep food safe to eat.

- Eat a variety of foods.
  Choose a diet low in saturated fat and cholesterol
      and moderate in total fat.
  Choose beverages and foods that limit your intake of sugars.
  Choose and prepare foods with less salt.
  If you drink alcoholic beverages, do so in moderation.

What you eat plays a very important role in a healthy eating plan. But, as you'll see in the next section, it's not the whole picture. Just as important as what you eat is how much you eat. It's also one of the most overlooked aspects of a healthy meal plan.

Fad Diets? Stay off the Bandwagon!

They seem to be everywhere. Quick-fix diets, nutritional supplements, and weight-loss programs, all promising the same thing—dramatic weight loss in a short amount of time. Sounds too good to be true? Well, it is. Many new, fad diets are not only ineffective over the long term, but some can also be very bad for your health—especially if you have diabetes.

Meal planning is an essential part of proper diabetes management and good health. You need to eat a variety of foods. Straying from this plan to drop a few pounds (that will soon come back) can do more damage than good. You could get better results from measuring your servings so you eat the correct amount of food and taking a 20-minute walk each day.

Simple changes work, not "lifestyle shock" that makes diets impossible to stay on. You may get results from moving so dramatically from your original way of living, but you can't stay that way for long. You need to learn to eat in a way that you can live with. That's why most diets fail. Before long, the weight you lost so quickly (most often lost water weight, as opposed to real fat loss) will be right back on, and then some.

So the next time all your friends are trying to lose weight by eating hamburgers without the bun or slathering everything in a strange oriental mustard, stay off the fad diet bandwagon. A month later, when they're all back where they started, you'll be glad you did.

Serving Size Counts

Probably the biggest problem with any meal plan is the size of the servings. You can count calories, carbs, fats, or any other nutrient all you want, but if you're actually eating three times the amount you think you're eating, you're not going to get where you want to go.

The problem is that what most people consider a serving is not the recommended serving. This is a jumbo-sized country with jumbo-sized servings. For example, let's say you're following a meal plan that includes a baked potato for lunch (complete with all the fixings). The baked potato should probably fit nicely into the palm of your hand. The baked potato you will probably eat, however, will be twice that size. This gives you double the carbohydrate and calories. Furthermore, if you're adding fixings, you'll be adding double the fixings, giving you twice the fat, carbohydrate, and protein they provide. Eating too much healthy food is still eating too much.

The right size of meat servings is also a problem. The food pyramid suggests you have 2 to 3 servings of meat a day. But how much meat is in a serving? The answer is probably quite a bit different than you expect. A serving of meat is between 2 and 3 ounces, or about the size of a deck of cards. That means you should get about 5 to 7 ounces of meat a day. Unfortunately, you can get this much meat in one cheeseburger. You also need to be aware of how much fat is in the meat you're eating. Choosing more lean meats like turkey or fish will improve your health dramatically.

Serving size is especially important for people with diabetes. Eating double the carbohydrates in your meal plan can blow your blood sugar sky high. Gladys uses Equal® sweetener in many of her recipes as a great way to reduce excess calories and carbohydrate. She loves the light, sweet taste Equal adds (and the fact that a packet of Equal has 0 calories!).

How Much Is Too Much?

How can you remember proper serving sizes? Get out your cereal bowl, dinner plate, and drinking glass. Using measuring cups and a scale, put the correct serving of cereal in the bowl. Look at it. Put correct servings of meat, potatoes or rice, and vegetables on your plate. Look at it. Then fill your glass with the correct serving of milk, juice, or water. Cut a piece of pie or cake that has the right number of carbs for your meal plan and look at it. Train your eyes to help you eat the right servings.

Natural Metabolism Booster

You don't eat three meals a day? No problem. Eating small amounts of healthy food (healthy is the key word) throughout the day is a great way to boost your metabolism. It breaks up the amount of carbohydrate that you eat in a day into short bursts, so it doesn't raise your blood sugar so high or get stored as fat. Eating small amounts even helps to make your stomach smaller, allowing you to get full on less food.

But what about sit-down meals with the family? For all of us, just as in Gladys' family, these dinners provide a strong social connection that can nurture us more than just physically. However, you still don't want to eat too much in one sitting. Eat slowly so you'll know when you're getting full. It takes 15 minutes for that message to get from your stomach to your brain, so make the pleasure of eating last. Take your time.

Cheating?

In this chapter we've discussed a lot of the ways you can achieve a healthy eating plan. We've talked about Al's simple rule. We've talked about what you should eat and how much of it you should eat. We've even talked about *how* you should eat. All of these are a part of Gladys' recipe for living a healthier lifestyle, a recipe she loves and follows religiously. But not all the time. It's this last ingredient that Gladys seems to love the best, and she's pretty sure you will, too.

From time to time, Gladys says, she "cheats." One day she will eat too many cookies or another day she doesn't get up and exercise—she takes a little break from the schedule. She lets her hair down. And she knows that this "cheating" gives her the motivation to keep on with her healthy lifestyle. When you try to be too rigid and forbid yourself to eat certain things, then you think you've ruined your whole plan when you eat something you think you shouldn't and you quit trying. Gladys is a wise woman. Her cheating is actually just taking a break from time to time—and it works.

There's No Such Thing As Cheating Anymore

But guess what? Even for people with diabetes, there's no such thing as cheating anymore. We now know that your body treats all sources of carbohydrate the same way—a brownie and a baked potato both raise your blood sugar to about the same level. As far as your blood sugar level is concerned, there's little difference. You can have the brownie when you work it into your meal plan as one of your carb foods. You can trade it for a roll or a serving of rice or noodles. As long as you know the carb count in each food, and know how many carbs you need to eat in a meal or snack, you can substitute the brownie for the baked potato. Just don't do it every day—because it will affect your weight and give you too many "empty calories." Keep track of your carb, calorie, and fat totals for the day. A registered dietitian can show you how to do this.

Knowing you can fit sweets and other favorite foods into a healthy meal plan makes you feel less deprived—and more willing to commit to a healthy lifestyle. It works for Gladys. Why? Because eating some of her favorite foods once in awhile helps her stick with her meal plan.

"Having a structured plan for eating is good and all, but every once in awhile I just need to slip in a little something [special]. Just to keep from going crazy. And that's important. If you can't live with what you're doing, you're not going to stick with it."

She's right. Eating healthy foods is great, but every once in awhile you're going to get an urge for something sinfully rich and calorie-laden that doesn't fit well into your normal meal plan. Chocolate tastes good, ice cream tastes good, pie tastes good. It's almost inevitable that you're going to give into your urges. It's natural. The problem is, with most diets and lifestyle plans, these foods are strictly off limits, and this creates a negative mindset. When certain foods are forbidden, you feel that if you eat these foods, you've broken the program. So you abandon your eating plan. Suddenly, it seems you have to give up your lifestyle just to have a bowl of ice cream.

Look at Gladys. She is very good about sticking to her plan and making sure she gets the food and exercise she needs. But she's only human, and every once in awhile she has some pretty strong cravings for some Häagen Dazs ice cream. So, instead of chucking her plan and calling it quits, she goes ahead and has a bowl. Then, she returns to her regular plan. She realizes that for any plan to work, it has to be flexible.

Of course, when we say occasional treats, we don't mean three-day benders of stuffing and gorging. But having a piece of birthday cake isn't going to destroy what you've worked so hard to build. If you have diabetes, trade the carbs in the cake for the roll and rice at dinner to keep your blood sugar down and enjoy. You'll find that including some of your favorite foods in your meal plan will make it much easier for you to enjoy your new healthy lifestyle!

Putting It All Together

Now that you've seen Gladys' and Al's plan for healthy eating, it's time to move on to the second prong of the two pronged attack—exercise. Before we move on, it might be best to cover the basics once again. When working on a meal plan, remember:

- "If you can't wash it, don't eat it!"
- Curb your cravings and try to trim back on fats.
- Make your eating plan livable for you.
- Use the food pyramid as a guide.
- Try to follow your daily meal plan.
- Serving size counts!
- Instead of a couple of big meals, eat small meals throughout the day.
- Favorite foods are okay—just account for them in your daily carb, calorie, and fat totals.

CHAPTER FOUR

Burn, Calories, Burn!

On the Treadmill to Personal Success

L ooking good is not the only reason Gladys exercises daily. She wants to be as healthy as she can, sing as well as she can, and enjoy her children and grandchildren for as long as she can. Every fitness expert will tell you that exercise is an essential part of any healthy living plan. Food choices are very important, but with exercise, you'll find you get faster weight-loss results and long-term success. Exercise is also the way to avoid a host of health problems such as heart disease, high blood pressure, and especially diabetes. In fact, there's such a strong link between lack of exercise and the development of diabetes that diabetes is being called an exercise-deficiency disorder. If you have diabetes (or you're a high-risk candidate looking to stave off the possibility of diabetes in the future), exercise is the most fundamental ingredient in your recipe to better health.

Why Is Exercise So Important?

Many people believe that just by adjusting their diet, they can achieve rapid weight loss and massive benefits to their health in a relatively short period of time. And who can blame them? Our society is saturated with quick-fix diets that promise to melt the pounds away and leave you trimmer and fitter, just by eating a certain combination of foods or taking some strange herbal supplements. Gladys herself has fallen for a number of these quick-fix solutions. As we've discussed earlier, these fad diets usually don't produce, sending you right back to where you started from. But there's another reason dieting alone usually doesn't keep the weight off for good. It all goes back to your body's chemistry.

Get up and get moving!

When you starve yourself of nutrients and calories (like all extreme diets do), you lose water, so you lose weight. This is what makes many fad diets appear successful after only a week or so. You can lose up to ten pounds of water weight quickly, and when you step on the scale it looks like the pounds are dropping away. Actually, you haven't lost any real weight at all. As the weeks go on, you don't lose any more weight, while at the same time, your desire to eat more food grows stronger. Finally—and it's happened to everybody—you give in and the diet's over.

So what does this have to do with exercise? Everything. When you exercise, you burn calories from the food you eat. When you've used those up, your body's going to burn fat. When you've exercised enough to build some muscle, the newly developed muscle burns calories even when you're not doing anything. How cool is that? You get double value for your effort. Pretty soon, you'll be a well-running machine.

Exercise and Diabetes

The best medicine for diabetes is to embark upon a healthy lifestyle. In fact, that's the first thing most doctors prescribe—

a meal plan and some regular exercise. Not only do these two lifestyle changes help keep diabetes under control, they can actually work to reverse the effects diabetes has on your body.

Regular exercise is your best bet for looking and feeling great. Just look at Gladys! Besides keeping your diabetes in good shape, exercise can:

- help you lose weight
- improve your appearance
- relieve stress and anxiety
- improve your sex life
- give you more energy
- improve your self-image
- lower your levels of cholesterol and lipids
- improve your blood pressure
- strengthen your heart and lungs
- impress your friends (and your fans)
- significantly reduce your chances of developing heart disease and other serious conditions

So it's obvious, exercise is good stuff. But, like most things, it's a lot easier said than done.

When Al Met Gladys

Like most of us, Gladys had lived most of her life with a minor aversion to exercise. In high school, she ran track and was a cheerleader. But after graduation, she didn't spend any more time in the gym or running circles around the track. Her life was constantly on the go with her budding stardom and the task of juggling family and career. When Al came into her life 9 years ago with a plan for fitness and health, he realized that structured exercise was going to be foreign for her. He knew he would have to make small changes and work exercise in slowly, until being active became almost second nature to Gladys.

The biggest problem was that Gladys' body had become accustomed to living a certain way. She could get up on stage and dance and sing, but that was about all the activity her body did. She could handle the exertion these activities called for, but her body wasn't ready to do anything else. Thus, when the newly motivated Gladys would get on a health kick and head to the gym to work out for an hour and a half, her body would seem to punish her. The workout would hurt, she'd be out of breath, and for the next two to three days, she'd be amazingly sore. Overall, the experience would be so unpleasant that she wouldn't want to repeat the activity, associating exercise with discomfort and pain. Luckily, Al knew how to change all of that.

Start Slow and Avoid Lifestyle Shock

Just as Gladys did, the most universal mistake people starting a workout plan make is doing too much too quickly. If you live a sedentary lifestyle, your body's going to be completely unprepared for vigorous exercise, and you're going to suffer a lifestyle shock. After a pretty uncomfortable workout, your body will do just what Gladys' did—punish you. Suddenly, you'll only think of pain and suffering when you think of the gym, and probably do your best to avoid going back.

Talk to Your Physician

Before starting any workout plan, it's important to talk to your physician and get a physical exam. He or she can determine the shape that you're in and recommend activities that will suit your health needs and lifestyle. For example, if you have a heart condition, high impact aerobics may not be the best activity for you, at least not to start with. Likewise, if you have diabetes, you have to be careful with your feet, so long-distance running might pose some serious health risks. You need to be aware of these conditions so you don't cause yourself any problems.

The most important thing to remember is to *start slowly*—even if you used to get plenty of exercise in the past and you're just trying to get back into the groove. Don't try to start where you left off. Ease your way in. This will make the experience more enjoyable and will help you stick with the program. What does starting slowly mean? To show you what we're talking about, let's use Gladys as an example.

Guidelines for Safe Exercise for People with Diabetes

If you have diabetes, there are some special precautions you should take when performing any type of exercise routine. When exercising, keep the following guidelines in mind. If you are already enjoying exercise, you may want to contact the International Diabetic Athletes Association to find out what activities and information they might have for you.

- Carry an identification card and wear a bracelet, necklace, or tag at all times that identifies you as having diabetes.
- Be alert for the signs of hypoglycemia during and for up to 12 hours after exercise. Sometimes exercise will affect your blood glucose the next day.
- Always carry a source of carbohydrate (such as glucose tablets) to treat hypoglycemia.
- If your fasting blood glucose is above 300 mg/dl before you exercise, do not exercise until your glucose is below 240 mg/dl and under control.
- Drink fluids before, after, and, if necessary, during exercise to prevent dehydration.

If you use insulin

- Avoid exercise when your insulin is working hardest (its peak action time).
- Don't inject insulin in an arm or a leg you'll be exercising, because activity will increase the blood flow and cause the insulin to be absorbed faster than usual.
- Your insulin dose may need to be decreased. Check with your health care team about making adjustments for your needs.

Guidelines for Safe Exercise (continued)

For type 1 diabetes, decreasing insulin by 20 percent before exercise is usually enough to prevent hypoglycemia. For longer activity (such as long-distance cycling or backpacking), a decrease in total insulin dose by 30–50 percent may be necessary.

For type 2 diabetes, if only one injection of intermediate-acting insulin is usually given (NPH or Lente), decrease the dose by 30 percent. Or, it may be easier to shift to two or more injections per day, with or without adding short-acting insulin. If a combination of intermediate-acting and short-acting insulin is used, both doses may be decreased by up to 30 percent. Check with your health care team for the best ways to do this.

Making It Fun

The easiest way to engage in any activity program is to make it fun. Do something that you enjoy. For instance, Gladys and her daughter Kenya love to play tennis (they've even played a few matches with their hero, Martina Navratilova), so Al decided that would be a perfect way to start introducing more rigorous exercise into Gladys' day. They started off with 30 minutes or so of tennis and moved on from there. Before too long, Gladys was spending more time in the gym—time she enjoyed—and the workouts were not too tough or painful.

There are lots of fun activities you can try so you reap the benefits. Just a few include:

- walking
- hiking
- riding a bicycle
- swimming
- playing basketball
- playing tennis
- playing golf (that's without the cart, of course)
- gardening

And the list goes on. Basically, anything that gets you up and moving—and burning calories and fat—is good for your body. Try working toward a goal—it's the easiest way to develop a fitness plan that works for you. Your goal can be a stronger tennis serve, a better golf swing, or simply enjoying three 30-minute walks a week.

Every Little Bit Counts

You may not realize it, but almost any activity you do can be a way to burn calories and lose weight. Fidgeting around in your chair can burn more calories than just sitting does. Exercise doesn't have to be structured or vigorous to give you positive results. In other words, you don't have to spend four hours a day at the gym to see some significant improvement in your health and your appearance. Daily activities like chores and yard work count as exercise, too. Problem is, in today's society, we don't get a lot of everyday activity.

Everything in our society is geared towards making life easier. The technologies we take for granted keep us from doing a lot of the exercise our ancestors, and even our grandparents, did on a daily basis. Washing machines, elevators, remote controls, riding lawn mowers—the list goes on and on. All of these things have made life a little easier for us. Unfortunately, it's also a little less healthy, too. You can see the effects of these laborsaving devices every time you step on the scale.

To counteract an exercise-free environment, try adding exercise to your lifestyle in small ways. The table below suggests ways you can fit exercise into your daily routine simply.

TABLE 4-1 Add Some Exercise

Exercise-free Activity	Healthy Alternative
Taking the elevator or escalator.	Taking the stairs. (Try a couple of flights to start off with. Work up to more stairs as you get in better shape.)

TABLE 4-1 Add Some Exercise (continued)

Exercise-free Activity	Healthy Alternative
Driving your car just a couple of blocks.	If it's not too far, walk.
Parking close to your workplace or the store you're visiting.	Try parking farther away and walking the extra distance.
Pushing a few bags of groceries to the car in a cart.	Carrying the groceries out by yourself.
Hiring someone to do your yard work.	Getting out and doing the yard work yourself. Gardening is a great way to get a little extra exercise.
Using a riding lawn mower.	Using a push lawn mower (if your yard isn't too huge).
Watching TV	Since TV is completely passive, almost anything at all is better than watching TV, at least in terms of exercise. Reading burns more calories than sitting and watching TV. However, there are things you can do while watching TV, like yoga or lifting light weights.

The list could go on and on. It's up to you and your creativity. If you see a way to slip a little exercise into your daily routine, go ahead and do it. Bit by bit, it all adds up, and you'll start to see results you never expected.

How to Get Where You Need to Go

Basically, if you burn more calories than you take in, you're going to lose some weight. More specifically, you're going to lose one pound of weight for every 3,500 calories burned. Here is a chart showing how many calories you burn during a

TABLE 4-2 Calories Burned

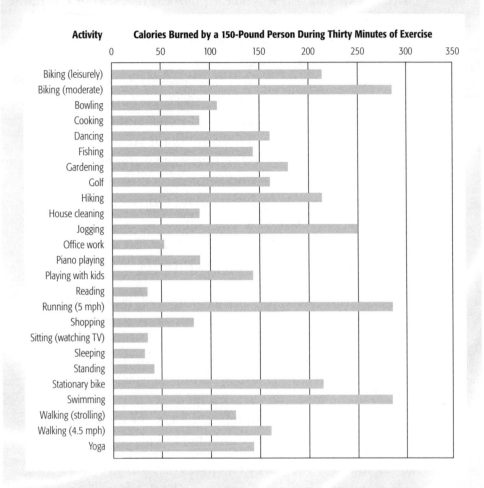

Activity	Calories Burned by a 150-Pound Person During Thirty Minutes of Exercise

The chart shows approximate calories burned (scale 0 to 350):

Activity	Calories Burned
Biking (leisurely)	~210
Biking (moderate)	~290
Bowling	~105
Cooking	~90
Dancing	~160
Fishing	~145
Gardening	~185
Golf	~160
Hiking	~215
House cleaning	~90
Jogging	~250
Office work	~55
Piano playing	~90
Playing with kids	~145
Reading	~40
Running (5 mph)	~285
Shopping	~85
Sitting (watching TV)	~40
Sleeping	~35
Standing	~45
Stationary bike	~215
Swimming	~285
Walking (strolling)	~130
Walking (4.5 mph)	~160
Yoga	~140

specific 30-minute exercise (for a 150-pound person). The amounts will be different according to your individual weight.

Many of these activities are excellent ways to burn calories, and what's more, they're all enjoyable and fun to do. If you don't enjoy what you're doing, you're not going to do it. The only successful routine that will work is the one that you will do. If you hate doing it, chances are, it's not going to last. But, if you stick with it, you'll soon find that you have much more energy than ever before. Hard to believe, isn't it? Well, it was hard for Gladys to believe, too. But now, she can't imagine a day without exercise.

And hey—give something different a shot. Yoga is rapidly gaining in popularity in the United States, even though it is a 5,000-year-old practice. There are lots of reasons for its popularity, but specifically it is a complete exercise program that is good for beginners, athletes, elders, pregnant women, and people with injuries or disabilities—in short, it's good for everyone. Yoga not only gives you flexibility and strength, it also lowers blood pressure and relieves stress. It would be best for you to start by taking a yoga class to be sure that your position in each posture is correct and to learn the breathing, which is very important. There are many yoga videos on the market—from catalogs to bookstores to Target stores—but we suggest you start with a good beginner's tape, such as the *Flowing Postures* series by Lilias Folan. Other excellent videos are the *Armchair Fitness Videos*.

Everything's Connected, Part II

Just as it is with diet, Al's approach to exercise is organic and natural. Not in the sense that he lifts heavy stones and chases down live prey with a slingshot, but in the sense of taking a holistic approach to well being. He believes that everything in our body is interconnected. So, when we start to exercise, we need to make sure that we work on every part of our body. Not only will this make for a healthier, safer workout, but it will also get some results in unexpected places.

For example, if you carry extra weight around your abdomen, your body will use lower back muscles to help out with the extra strain. These lower back muscles will then put strain on upper back and neck muscles. Pretty soon, having a little extra belly leads to poor posture, as well as back and neck pain.

With this in mind, you can see the importance of a total body workout. Often, we'll try to focus on one part of our body—like the abdomen—and neglect the rest. If you want to see results, work on the big picture, and you'll find that everything will fall into place much quicker with more dramatic results. This is the way Al's workout regimen for Gladys is designed, and it's the way that will work best for you.

Move on Down the Road—Al's Way

Al Claiborne is a big man, in obvious excellent shape. That's the thing about exercise—it shows when you practice what you preach. When he cracks his shy smile and begins to explain his system for getting into shape, his enthusiasm builds with real fire and carries you along. He loves being in great shape and he loves getting other people into great shape. It doesn't matter who you are, Al's confident he can get you to where you want to go. "If you're willing to do a little bit of work, I can make you look any way you want. It can happen." You believe every word he says because he's got the proof stacked all over him.

A Quick Evaluation

He takes you by the arm to stand in front of a full-length mirror to look at yourself honestly. Do you have to suck in your stomach and does it go right back out when you turn away or forget to hold it in? Is one shoulder higher than the other? He has you turn sideways, and asks you to check your posture. Can you draw a straight line from your ear to your hip, through your knee and ankle to the floor? He may touch your shoulder or waist to remind you where you need to straighten or let go. He asks you, then, to face the mirror again and slump forward looking down. Then he tells you to imagine a string going out of the top of your head, pulling you up like a puppet. When you follow the string and stand straight, your head goes up and your neck stretches longer. Press your shoulders down from your ears. Feel that your spine is straighter, and you can lift your rib cage. Your shoulders can drop even more. Take a deep breath and look. You're surprised to see that you have apparently just lost 5 pounds. Al jokes that he's going to save you shopping time and money, too. When you get into good physical shape, everything you put on looks good, so no more hours in the dressing room. Instead you're going to spend some happier hours walking, swimming, biking, and getting into good shape.

Back to the mirror, Al has you check that your hips are level and your knees are aligned. He points out that you should never lock your knees, but always have them just slightly bent.

He's checking your alignment, because many people have one leg shorter than the other and don't realize it. When they start walking or running, this can cause problems for their hip and knee joints. Now Al asks you to walk slowly toward the mirror. Do your feet turn out? If they do, you're only getting the distance from one side of your foot to the other, not from heel to toe. Al points out that you're going to have to take twice as many steps if you're only using half the length of your foot. Try to keep your toes straight ahead and let each step roll from heel around the outside of the foot up to the toe. With your head up, start walking slowly and mindfully around the room. Keep your shoulders relaxed and your stomach pulled in and centered in the cradle of your pelvis. Pay attention to where your weight is transferred to your feet. Feel the bottom of your foot as it touches the ground. "In the beginning of any exercise program it's important to get the basics down right," Al says. "Even if it's just walking. Then the more you walk or stand in the correct position, the more benefits you're going to get."

If you can, watch yourself walk in the mirror, or have someone watch you. (If you go to a local running shoe store, they'll watch you walk or run and give you feedback about your gait and what types of shoes will work best for you.) Do you lean backward or to one side? Does your gait seem smooth or awkward? Do you need to do stretches to loosen up the muscles in your legs and hips so you can move more smoothly?

Now Al has you check to see how flexible you are. You probably already know if you can bend over and pick something up, but go ahead and try. If your hands are still 12 inches from the floor, or your back is too stiff to do more than look like you might try to dive into the floor, then you need to do some stretching daily. In fact, everyone needs to do stretching daily. You will become more flexible as time goes by and put off or completely avoid the signs of aging that are actually just stiff muscles. You will also increase the benefits of any other exercise that you do if you add stretching.

Stretches can be called yoga, or Pilates, or tai chi. Stretches flow through dance classes and begin and end sports workouts. You can find stretches in books (try the library if you don't want to buy one), in magazines, on television shows, and on videos and audiotapes. Again, check at your library for exercise video and audiotapes. The nice thing about having so many places to find different exercise routines to try is that you can easily and inexpensively add variety to your routine. And variety is one of the reasons Gladys doesn't get bored and give up on her daily exercise. It will work for you, too.

A Simple, Powerful Plan

Al's plan for exercising for your life has three parts:

* Stretching
* Lifting light weights
* Aerobic exercise—working heart and lungs

Stretch. He suggests that you stretch every day. Watch your cat or dog. They always stretch after they wake up. You might try that and stretch before you get out of bed in the morning or in the bathroom before your shower. For longer or more intense stretches, be sure that your muscles are warmed up first. Swing your arms and march or jog in place first or stretch after you finish walking. Many people find that it is easier to stretch in the afternoon or evening.

Weights. Try to lift weights at least two times a week. Gladys aims for lifting weights or working with weight machines every other day. Al cautions you not to lift two days in a row, or if you do use weights every day, don't work the same sets of muscles two days in a row. You are breaking down muscle fibers to make stronger muscles, and they need a day to rest and heal. Don't lift heavy weights (more than 25 pounds) if you have high blood pressure or certain diabetic complications such as retinopathy. Ask your health care provider for help deciding what is best for you.

It would be great if you could have a session or two with a trainer like Al. Many YMCA's and community recreation centers have trained staff who can help you learn to lift weights correctly. If you must lift at home and you have limited funds, you can still do it and get all the great benefits of building muscle. Muscle burns calories (and blood sugar) even at rest. This is the main reason you want more muscle on your heavenly body. "Muscle strength helps you be independent—you can open any jar and amaze your children and grandchildren," says Gladys with a smile.

You can use 1-pound cans or plastic milk jugs filled with water as weights if you don't want to buy them. A simple weight routine—again, you can find them in magazines like *Men's Fitness* or *Self*, in books, or on videotapes (all available at your local library)—takes about 20 minutes and may surprise you. You may find that all your muscles feel a deep and gentle relaxation. If you find that you have difficulty getting to sleep, a session with your weights may be just what you need. You have to work a muscle before it can relax.

Aerobic exercise. As Al says, your choices are endless...from gardening to running a marathon. And the more ways you exercise, the more likely you are to keep doing it. You can walk, run, skate, swim, bike, hike, ride, row, paddle, sail, climb, and backpack—every activity but flying like a bird, but flapping your arms counts. The key is to do 30 minutes of an aerobic exercise that raises your heart rate and gets you breathing deeply. You can do it in 10-minute segments to fit into your schedule if you need to. Al and Gladys prefer to get 30 to 60 minutes of aerobic exercise a day, even if it is just a fast walk around the downtown area where she might be performing that night.

Gladys prefers to exercise mid-morning and to go from aerobics to weights to stretching and a cool down. It takes her about two hours and she has found that it makes her feel great physically and emotionally. In fact, it helps her on stage, too, giving her endurance to perform for hours and come back for three encores.

The daily exercise does more than help you drop pounds, too. It has, as you can see, helped Gladys to retain a youthful glow and trim body. She doesn't look like someone's grandmother, but she is and proud of it.

Once you feel you're ready to move on to bigger and better things, talk with your doctor about what structured exercises you're fit to do. Once you get the okay from your physician, consider going to the gym or taking some structured classes.

Most gyms have personal fitness instructors who can help you develop a workout plan that works best for you.

Tying It All Together

You now have two-thirds of Gladys Knight's recipe for better living, a recipe she uses to live life to the fullest. Some people may be a little disappointed that there's no strict regimen here, no exact formula detailing every single thing you need to do to lose weight fast, and keep it off. There's a reason for that. It's this kind of thinking that keeps many people from enjoying a long-lasting, healthy lifestyle. There is no "one size fits all" method for better fitness, no single theory that will apply to everybody who reads this book.

Every person is different, and every person will need to take a different path towards better health. What you need to do is find the path that works best for you, using the guidelines described here as your road map. Using a single diet or "scientifically designed" exercise plan is not going to get every one of us to that ultimate goal. What works for some people may not work for you. Whether it's because your body is built differently, you live on a different time schedule, or just because you don't enjoy an activity enough to stick with it over a long period of time, the same thing won't work for everybody. You have to do what works for you.

This is a big part of Gladys' recipe. She knows from first-hand experience that fad diets and strict eating programs may help you drop some pounds quickly, but the results never last. The only way to keep those pounds off for good, and keep your body in good shape, is to find a workout that you can live with. The best way to have a workout you enjoy is to create one yourself. You know yourself better than anyone else does, so you know what you like and what you will do. Thus, with a little education and an idea of what makes a healthy lifestyle, you're best suited to creating a fitness plan you like.

With all of these things in mind, you'll realize that a healthy attitude towards your lifestyle will reap the most rewards. You'll look better, you'll reduce your chances of developing some pretty nasty conditions (and if you have diabetes, you'll greatly improve the condition you're in), and most importantly, you'll feel better. Exercise is also your best prescription for one of the most common ailments in our society today—stress and anxiety. With proper diet and exercise, you'll find that your mood will improve ten-fold and that the youthful energy you thought you'd lost forever will be back in full force.

Of course, you'll never get any of these benefits if you don't stick with your program. Which leads us to the third and final ingredient of Gladys' recipe for better fitness—staying on track.

CHAPTER FIVE

Staying on Track

The Midnight Train to Better Living

In the span of just a few short years, Gladys Knight has seen her life transform in a number of ways. She's enjoying a renewed musical success she hasn't seen in years, her beautiful family is growing up right in front of her eyes, and most surprising to Gladys herself, she's enjoying a level of fitness she never thought she could attain. With the help of Al, and the support of her family, she's developed a healthy diet and an exercise routine that she enjoys. But the road to fitness was not an easy one, and along the way, Gladys has endured periods where she felt she just couldn't take it anymore. But she has always pulled herself up out of her rut and got back on track, and in this chapter, you'll learn ways you can do the same thing.

Gladys brings down the house after breaking out on her own.

Do It Your Way

By now, you're probably sick of hearing it, but the best way to ensure that you'll stick with your fitness program is to make it enjoyable. If it's not fun, or if it's downright unbearable, you're not going to do it. However, if you like what you're doing, if it's something you look forward to (maybe not right at the beginning, but eventually), then sticking with it will be no problem. You'll find that you make time, no matter how hectic your schedule, to fit in the things you like to do.

And stay away from programs that are too foreign to your lifestyle. Remember, dramatic changes are hard on your body and on your mind. Suddenly, you're enduring a lot of stress you're not used to, or you're in actual physical pain and discomfort. While the old adage "no pain, no gain" is suitable sometimes, it's the worst thing you can do when starting off. As you progress, you'll find that pushing yourself to do things you couldn't before will become second nature. But in the beginning, discomfort can be a strong deterrent. Push yourself to just get started and be a little more active with each passing day. The gain from pain will evolve naturally.

Reward Yourself

Another way to make sure you stick with the program is to reward yourself for a job well done. Getting your life fitness-friendly isn't easy, and your hard work deserves a little compensation. There are no set guidelines on how you should reward yourself—you know what you like best. But try to stay within the guidelines of a healthy lifestyle. If your reward for a week of working out is to not work out for the next two weeks, you've just eroded everything you tried to accomplish.

A good way to give a little back to yourself is to consider some of the luxuries you enjoy, and then only allow yourself to indulge when you accomplish certain goals. For instance, if you enjoy going out for a nice meal on the weekends, this could be considered a luxury. It's not necessary, and by cutting it out of your routine, the only thing you've lost is a little personal enjoyment. Therefore, tell yourself that you'll only allow yourself an evening out if you accomplish all of your fitness goals for the week. With the thought of a reward waiting for you at the end of the week, staying motivated will be no problem.

Some things to keep in mind when you reward yourself for adhering to your plan:

- Make the rewards meaningful.
- Make sure your rewards still fit within your fitness plan.
- Only reward yourself if you accomplish what you determined you would accomplish. If you indulge in your rewards anyway, they become meaningless.
- Only reward worthwhile accomplishments.
- Gradually build the accomplishments you reward. Remember, you're trying to move forward. Rewarding the same thing every week won't get you anywhere.

With these things in mind, try and determine what would get you motivated. Then, tell yourself that you'll only enjoy certain luxuries if you stick to your plan. Pretty soon, you'll find that getting exercise and feeling great can be reward enough. But until then, a little chocolate cake on the weekends or a trip to the movies can be a great way to keep you going.

Enlist the Help of Others

As with most things in life, getting in shape is much more fun, and less strenuous, when you do it with somebody else. Having others join in your quest for fitness can help keep you motivated and going. On those days when you feel like you just can't do it, some encouraging words from others can get you back on track.

The best way to get help from a fitness buddy is to find someone who already has a routine and ask if you can join in. That way, you're enlisting the help of somebody who is already motivated to a healthier lifestyle. Your buddy can share tips for sticking with the program that you're using, as well as provide proof positive of the benefits a healthy lifestyle can bring. You'll find that having an example to follow can be a big push in the right direction.

Having a loved one come on board can also be a big boost. If your spouse is a few apples short of a healthy bushel, ask him or her to join you in your quest for a better way of living. Leisurely activities like walking, riding bikes, or swimming tend to be much more enjoyable when you're sharing them with someone you love.

Gladys was lucky enough to have a personal trainer devoted to her fitness to keep her motivated when she was feeling a little lackadaisical. On those days when she was less than thrilled to hit the gym, Al kept her going. Being in superb physical shape, Al was also a perfect example of what she could accomplish if she just stuck with it. But just because you don't have your own personal trainer by your side doesn't mean you can't enjoy the benefits of one. One of the best things about joining a health club is the guidance and motivation you can get from a club trainer. Most gyms have professionals on staff to help you develop a program that works for you. They can make appointments to meet with you through the week, and when someone else is expecting you, it's much easier to get in gear.

Unfortunately, not all the feedback you get from others is positive. Sometimes the people in your life can bombard you with negative thoughts and discouraging words. It may be hard, but try your best to get away from negative people who can ridicule your attempts at bettering yourself. Try and find positive influences and immerse yourself in an environment that reflects and supports your desires. This is one of Gladys' most ardent pieces of advice.

"All my life I've run into people who were telling me that I can't do this or I'd never be able to do that. What you have to do is block these people out and get as far away from them as possible. If you're constantly hearing that you can't do the things you were born to do, pretty soon, you're going to believe it."

Remember, a Little Food Flexibility Can Go a Long Way

Just like we talked about in chapter 3, including some of your favorite foods in your regular meal plan can help you stick with your program. Indulge yourself every once in a while and you'll find that living a healthy lifestyle doesn't have to be torture. If you want, make one serving of your favorite dessert a reward for accomplishing your weekly fitness goal. But remember, indulge in moderation and make the appropriate adjustments in your meal plan. Gladys carries Equal® sweetener in her purse to use during the day. But she does treat herself every once in awhile to keep from going crazy. As she says, "I love Haagen Daz ice cream. I can't help it . . . every once in a while, I just have to have some!"

Try Vanity—It's Amazingly Effective

Most of us hate to admit it, but it's true. Warding off risks to our health is inspiring and all, but for many of us, the real motivation to cut calories and hit the treadmill isn't a reduced risk of heart attack and stroke, it's so we can look good in a swimsuit. And there's nothing wrong with this, if it gets you up from the couch and into the gym.

Every day we're bombarded with images of beautiful people with beautiful bodies, and we want those bodies, too. However, many more people don't look like this than do. The good news is, by correcting your diet and getting some exercise, there's a good chance that you can get into the best shape of your life and look like you never imagined you could look. You may not be hitting any runways anytime soon, but a healthy lifestyle can get you a figure you've dreamed about. And nothing's more motivational than dropping your spouse's jaw or getting a compliment on how good you look.

Gladys is a little ashamed to admit it, but vanity keeps her going back to the gym for more every week. Of course, looking good is part of her career, and there was a time, not long ago, when she wasn't too confident about her appearance. Imagine standing in front of thousands of people in an evening gown under bright, unforgiving lights and thinking to yourself, "Oh my god, I can't believe how fat I look." It starts to wear on a person, and it had quite an effect on Gladys. Finally, she decided that she was sick of living with extra weight. She was going to look good in an evening dress, no matter what it took. Now, she looks better than she has in years and she couldn't be happier.

"I decided long ago that I was never going to be a stick-thin super model. I'm just not built that way. But I also realized that didn't mean I had to be overweight. Now, I'm a mother, and a grandmother, and I look and feel better than I have in a long time. It sounds bad, but being just a little bit vain, just a little bit, has kept me going in times when nothing else would."

A Long, Wonderful Road

You ask most people how they're doing and you're probably going to get a dismissive, "Oh, I'm doing fine." You ask Gladys and she'll tell you with an honest smile that she's never been happier in her entire life. In what most people consider to be the autumn of their life, Gladys has finally achieved the life she's always dreamed of. Maintaining a perfect balance of family, career success, and personal fulfillment, she looks forward to every day with an enthusiasm that's rare.

And why shouldn't she be happy? Her youthful appearance concealing the years of trials and tribulations she's endured, she's looking and feeling better than she could ever imagine. Her career has once again taken off in wonderful and unexpected directions. Her new album *At Last*, her first solo studio project in eight years, has been released by MCA records. Her family members, many of whom are intimately involved with

Sidney Poitier charms Gladys at her *50 Years in Show Business* anniversary celebration in 1999.

her career, are with her almost every day. Just recently, she unexpectedly found a new love in a long-time fan who just happened to meet her at the right place at the right time. Everything seems to be going right for the little girl from Atlanta with the big, beautiful voice.

Sitting on her couch in her spacious home in Henderson, Nevada, Gladys vivaciously tells the story of her life and her recipe for personal success. You can't help but enjoy every word she says, because behind each word you're hoping to find the key to living the life she's lived, and attaining the happiness she enjoys—the happiness that so many don't find. It's there. Behind every word and every story and every genial laugh lies the secret to her amazing life. It's simply love—love for family, love for staying healthy, love for enjoying everything that you do. Simply put, it's love for being alive.

So as you sit and you listen, you realize that right next to you is the most influential motivation of all. And as she smiles her contagious smile, you make a promise to yourself that from this day on, you'll live the life you want to live.

CHAPTER SIX

Recipes for Better Living

★ *Appetizers & Dips*

Fresh Herb Dip

Serves 12

Serving size: 2 Tbsp

Preparation time: 10 minutes

Exchanges
Free Food

Calories. 22
   Calories from Fat 2
Total Fat . . . . 0 g
   Saturated Fat. . . . . 0 g
Cholesterol. . . . . 1 mg
Sodium . . . . 134 mg
Carbohydrate. . . . . 2 g
   Dietary Fiber . . . . 0 g
   Sugars . . . . 2 g
Protein . . . . 3 g

3/4 cup fat-free yogurt
  1 cup low-fat cottage cheese, small curd
  1 tsp lime juice
  2 tsp finely grated onion
  1 tsp minced fresh dill
  1 tsp minced fresh thyme
  1 tsp minced fresh oregano
  1 tsp minced fresh basil
  1 tsp rice vinegar
1/4 tsp salt

1 Combine ingredients in a blender and blend until smooth. Cover and refrigerate until chilled.

Smothered Chicken Drumlets

Serves 5

Serving size: 3 drumlets

Preparation time: 20 minutes

Exchanges
1/2 Carbohydrate
2 Medium-Fat Meat

Calories	197
Calories from Fat	92
Total Fat	10 g
Saturated Fat	3 g
Cholesterol	71 mg
Sodium	392 mg
Carbohydrate	8 g
Dietary Fiber	2 g
Sugars	5 g
Protein	18 g

15 chicken drumlets
1 cup orange juice
1 Tbsp Worcestershire sauce
1 tsp curry
1 tsp black pepper
1 Tbsp seasoning salt
1/8 tsp cayenne pepper
1 Tbsp light olive oil
1 garlic clove, minced
1 onion, sliced
1/2 red bell pepper, sliced
1/2 yellow bell pepper, sliced
1/2 green bell pepper, sliced
1 cup sliced mushrooms

1 Wash drumlets in a bowl of cool water. Drain and set aside.

2 In a large flat dish, mix the orange juice, Worcestershire sauce, curry, black pepper, seasoning salt, and cayenne pepper. Place the drumlets in the marinade, cover, and refrigerate 40 minutes to 2 hours.

3 Heat the oil over medium-high heat in a large skillet. Add the garlic and vegetables and sauté about 1 minute. Add the drumlets and brown on both sides, about 5 minutes on each side.

4 Turn the heat down to medium, cover, and cook for 15–20 minutes, turning chicken occasionally until drumlets are no longer pink.

Snack Mix

Serves 10

Serving size: 1 cup

Preparation time: 15 minutes

Exchanges
1 Starch
1/2 Fat

Calories 90
   Calories from Fat 26
Total Fat . . . . 3 g
   Saturated Fat . . . . 1 g
Cholesterol . . . . 6 mg
Sodium . . . . 157 mg
Carbohydrate . . . . 15 g
   Dietary Fiber . . . . 2 g
   Sugars . . . . 2 g
Protein . . . . 2 g

6 cups plain air-popped popcorn
1 cup Rice Chex cereal
1 cup Cheerios cereal
1 cup Bran Chex cereal
1 cup mini pretzel sticks
2 Tbsp butter, melted
1/2 tsp garlic powder
1/2 tsp onion powder
1 cup cashews (optional)

1 Preheat oven to 300°F. Combine the first five ingredients and cashews (if using).

2 Drizzle melted butter over the mixture. Sprinkle with garlic powder and onion powder and mix well. Put the mixture in a shallow pan and spread into a single layer.

3 Bake for 10 minutes. Stir a few times during baking. Turn off the oven and let the mixture cool in the oven. Store in an airtight container.

Spicy Apple Salsa

Serves 6

Serving size: 1/4 cup

Preparation time: 15 minutes

Exchanges
Free Food

Calories 14
   Calories from Fat 1
Total Fat . . . . 0 g
   Saturated Fat . . . . 0 g
Cholesterol . . . . 0 mg
Sodium . . . . 36 mg
Carbohydrate . . . . 4 g
   Dietary Fiber . . . . 1 g
   Sugars . . . . 3 g
Protein . . . . 0 g

   1 cup diced Granny Smith apples
1/4 cup diced red bell pepper
1/4 cup diced red onion
   1 Tbsp chopped fresh cilantro
1 1/2 tsp minced jalapeño pepper
1/2 tsp grated lime rind
1/8 tsp salt
1 1/2 Tbsp fresh lime juice
1/8 tsp black pepper
   1 small garlic clove, minced

1 Combine all ingredients in a bowl and mix well. Serve with baked tortilla chips or pork chops.

Spinach Squares

Serves 8

Serving size: 2 squares

Preparation time: 20 minutes

Exchanges
1 Lean Meat

Calories.............. 50
   Calories from Fat 14
Total Fat .... 2 g
   Saturated Fat.......... 1 g
Cholesterol........... 30 mg
Sodium .... 180 mg
Carbohydrate........... 3 g
   Dietary Fiber.......... 1 g
   Sugars .... 1 g
Protein .... 6 g

1 10-oz pkg frozen chopped spinach, thawed
1/8 tsp nutmeg
1 cup low-fat cottage cheese, small curd
2 tsp all-purpose flour
2 Tbsp grated Parmesan cheese
1 egg yolk
1/8 tsp black pepper
1/8 tsp cayenne pepper
2 egg whites

1 Preheat the oven to 400°F. Line the bottom of an 8 × 8 square pan with wax paper and set aside. Lightly squeeze the thawed spinach and place in a large bowl. Add the nutmeg.

2 Place the cottage cheese in a blender and blend for 30 seconds. Add the flour, Parmesan cheese, egg yolk, black pepper, and cayenne pepper. Process an additional 30 seconds or until well blended. Add the blender contents to the spinach mixture and stir well.

3 In a small bowl, beat the egg whites until they form stiff peaks. Gently fold into the spinach mixture. Pour the mixture into the baking pan. Bake, uncovered, for 20 minutes or until set and golden.

4 Place the pan on a wire rack and cool for 5 minutes. Slice into 16 squares and serve warm.

Wings to Fly By

Serves 4

Serving size: 2 wings

Preparation time: 10 minutes

Exchanges
3 Medium-Fat Meat
1/2 Fat

Calories	243
Calories from Fat	148
Total Fat	16 g
Saturated Fat	5 g
Cholesterol	66 mg
Sodium	359 mg
Carbohydrate	2 g
Dietary Fiber	0 g
Sugars	2 g
Protein	20 g

8 chicken wings
1/4 cup Worcestershire sauce
1 tsp salt-free garlic herb seasoning
1 whole onion, halved, then sliced
1 tsp sage
1 tsp butter
1 bay leaf
1/8 tsp black pepper
1 tsp seasoning salt
1/2 cup cider vinegar
1 tsp olive oil

1 Wash the wings under cool running water. Drain and set aside.

2 In a large flat dish, mix together all ingredients except the olive oil. Add the wings to the marinade, cover, and refrigerate 30 minutes to 2 hours.

3 Heat the oil over medium heat in a large skillet. Add the wings and brown on both sides, about 5 minutes on each side.

4 Lower the heat to medium low and cook for about 20 minutes or until the meat is tender and falls easily off the bone.

Yogurt Cheese Dip

Serves 16

Serving size: 1 Tbsp

Preparation time: 5 minutes

Exchanges
Free Food

Calories 17
   Calories from Fat 2
Total Fat . . . . 0 g
   Saturated Fat. . . . . 0 g
Cholesterol. . . . . 0 g
Sodium . . . . 10 mg
Carbohydrate. . . . . 3 g
   Dietary Fiber . . . . 0 g
   Sugars . . . . 2 g
Protein . . . . 1 g

2 cups plain fat-free yogurt
2 Tbsp chopped raisins
1 Tbsp chopped pecans
1/4 tsp EQUAL® for Recipes **or**
1 packet EQUAL® sweetener **or**
2 tsp EQUAL® Spoonful™
1 tsp grated orange rind

1 Line a sieve with a double layer of cheesecloth that has been rinsed out and squeezed dry. Allow the cheesecloth to overlap at the sides.

2 Stir the yogurt until smooth and pour into the sieve. Fold edges of cheesecloth over to cover yogurt. Place the sieve in a large pan and refrigerate 12–24 hours.

3 Remove the yogurt from the sieve (discard the liquid) and place in a medium bowl. Add the remaining ingredients and stir well. Refrigerate 8 hours to allow the flavors to blend.

4 Spoon into a serving bowl and serve with assorted fresh fruits for dipping.

★ *Beverages*

Banana Strawberry Smoothie

Serves 5

Serving size: 1 cup

Preparation time: 5 minutes

Exchanges
2 Fruit

Calories 119
   Calories from Fat 3
Total Fat . . . . 0 g
   Saturated Fat. . . . . 0 g
Cholesterol. . . . . 0 mg
Sodium . . . . 3 mg
Carbohydrate . . . . 30 g
   Dietary Fiber. . . . . 3 g
   Sugars . . . . 24 g
Protein . . . . 1 g

2 medium-size very ripe bananas, cut into small chunks and frozen
2 cups strawberries, frozen
2 cups orange juice
1/2 tsp EQUAL® for Recipes **or**
1 1/2 packets EQUAL® sweetener **or**
1 Tbsp EQUAL® Spoonful™
1/2 Tbsp lemon juice

1 Place all ingredients in a blender and process until smooth.

Chocolate Almond Smoothie

Serves 2

Serving size: 1 cup

Preparation time: 5 minutes

Exchanges
2 1/2 Carbohydrate

Calories	187
Calories from Fat	0
Total Fat	0 g
Saturated Fat	0 g
Cholesterol	2 mg
Sodium	151 mg
Carbohydrate	40 g
Dietary Fiber	0 g
Sugars	36 g
Protein	7 g

1 cup fat-free vanilla frozen yogurt
3/4 cup fat-free, lactose-free milk
2 Tbsp chocolate syrup
1/8 tsp almond extract
1/8 tsp vanilla extract

1 Combine all ingredients in a blender and blend until smooth.

Peachy Treat

Serves 2

Serving size: 1 cup

Preparation time: 5 minutes

Exchanges
2 Fruit

Calories. 133
   Calories from Fat 2
Total Fat . . . . 0 g
   Saturated Fat. . . . . 0 g
Cholesterol. . . . . 0 mg
Sodium . . . . 15 mg
Carbohydrate . . . . 34 g
   Dietary Fiber. . . . . 4 g
   Sugars . . . . 23 g
Protein . . . . 1 g

1 cup peaches (sliced fresh
   or unsweetened frozen)
1 cup apricot nectar
1 Tbsp fresh orange juice
1/4 cup carrot juice
1 to 2 scoops soy protein powder
   (optional)
1 tsp psyllium fiber

1 Mix all ingredients in a blender for one minute or until smooth.

Pumpkin Smoothie

Serves 1

Serving size: 1 3/4 cups

Preparation time: 5 minutes

Exchanges
2 1/2 Carbohydrate

Calories	159
Calories from Fat	5
Total Fat	1 g
Saturated Fat	0 g
Cholesterol	3 mg
Sodium	85 mg
Carbohydrate	35 g
Dietary Fiber	4 g
Sugars	25 g
Protein	6 g

1/2 cup pumpkin, canned
1/4 tsp cinnamon
1/8 tsp nutmeg
1/2 cup chilled apple juice
1/4 cup fat-free milk
1/4 cup fat-free vanilla yogurt
3 ice cubes

1 Combine all ingredients in a blender and blend until smooth. Serve cold. Garnish with a cinnamon stick, if desired.

Zingy Tropical Surprise

Serves 2

Serving size: 1 cup

Preparation time: 5 minutes

Exchanges
2 1/2 fruit

Calories 161
   Calories from Fat 4
Total Fat . . . . 0 g
   Saturated Fat . . . . 0 g
Cholesterol . . . . 1 mg
Sodium . . . . 25 mg
Carbohydrate . . . . 39 g
   Dietary Fiber . . . . 2 g
   Sugars . . . . 31 g
Protein . . . . 3 g

1 cup unsweetened pineapple juice
1/4 cup fresh lemon or orange juice
1 large ripe frozen banana
2 Tbsp fat-free dry milk powder
4 ice cubes

1 Combine ingredients in a blender. Cover and blend on high speed until fully mixed and frothy.

★ Salads

California Cobb Salad

Serves 4

Serving size: 1/4 recipe

Preparation time: 15 minutes

Exchanges
3 Lean Meat
2 Vegetable
1 Fat

Calories 261
    Calories from Fat 131
Total Fat . . . . 15 g
    Saturated Fat . . . . 5 g
Cholesterol . . . . 259 mg
Sodium . . . . 417 mg
Carbohydrate . . . . 8 g
    Dietary Fiber . . . . 3 g
    Sugars . . . . 3 g
Protein . . . . 25 g

1 head red lettuce, chopped
4 hard-boiled eggs, chopped
1/4 cup chopped black olives
2 chicken breast halves, cooked and diced
4 pieces bacon, pre-cooked and crumbled
1/4 cup aged blue cheese
1/2 cup minced yellow and red peppers
1 tomato, minced

1 Place the lettuce on 4 plates. From right to left around the plate, place the eggs, olives, chicken, bacon, blue cheese, peppers, and tomato. Serve with salad dressing of choice.

Carrot & Apple Salad

Serves 5

Serving size: 1 2/3 cups

Preparation time: 25 minutes

Exchanges
2 Vegetable
1 Fruit

Calories 107
   Calories from Fat 4
Total Fat . . . . 0 g
   Saturated Fat . . . . 0 g
Cholesterol . . . . 0 mg
Sodium . . . . 189 mg
Carbohydrate . . . . 26 g
   Dietary Fiber . . . . 4 g
   Sugars . . . . 18 g
Protein . . . . 2 g

  1 medium red pepper, thinly sliced
1/4 cup seedless raisins
     (dark or golden)
  2 Tbsp cider vinegar
  1 tsp cinnamon
1/2 tsp EQUAL® for Recipes **or**
1 1/2 packets EQUAL® sweetener **or**
  1 Tbsp EQUAL® Spoonful™
1/4 cup fat-free mayonnaise
  1 Tbsp Dijon mustard
1/8 tsp black pepper
  1 medium Red Delicious apple,
     unpeeled and thinly sliced
 16 oz shredded carrots

1 In a 1-quart saucepan over high heat, heat the red pepper, raisins, cider vinegar, and cinnamon to boiling. Reduce the heat to low and simmer, uncovered, 3–5 minutes or until the red pepper is tender.

2 Remove the saucepan from the heat. Stir in the Equal®, mayonnaise, Dijon mustard, and black pepper.

3 Place the apple and carrots in a medium bowl. Add the contents of the saucepan and toss well.

Chicken Curry Salad

Serves 4

Serving size: 1/4 recipe

Preparation time: 15 minutes

Exchanges
4 Lean Meat
1 1/2 Fruit
1 Fat

Calories 361
  Calories from Fat 160
Total Fat . . . . 18 g
  Saturated Fat . . . . 3 g
Cholesterol . . . . 78 mg
Sodium . . . . 443 mg
Carbohydrate . . . . 24 g
  Dietary Fiber . . . . 2 g
  Sugars . . . . 17 g
Protein . . . . 27 g

1 lb boneless, skinless chicken
  breast, cooked and diced
2 tsp mustard
1/2 cup lite mayonnaise
1/2 cup chopped celery
1/2 onion, finely minced
1 apple, peeled and chopped
1/4 cup chopped walnuts
1/2 cup raisins
1 tsp seasoning salt
1/2 tsp curry powder
1/8 tsp pepper

1 Combine all ingredients in a large bowl and toss to mix. Chill before serving.

Chicken Peanut Salad

Serves 4

Serving size: 1/4 recipe

Preparation time: 20 minutes

Exchanges
1/2 Carbohydrate
3 Lean Meat

Calories. 209
   Calories from Fat 94
Total Fat . . . . 10 g
   Saturated Fat. . . . . 2 g
Cholesterol. . . . . 62 mg
Sodium . . . . 405 mg
Carbohydrate. . . . . 6 g
   Dietary Fiber . . . . 1 g
   Sugars . . . . 3 g
Protein . . . . 23 g

2 Tbsp peanut butter
2 Tbsp lite soy sauce
2 Tbsp cider vinegar
1 tsp sesame oil
1 1/2 tsp minced fresh ginger
   (or 1/4 tsp ground ginger)
1 clove garlic, minced
1/8 tsp cayenne pepper
2 cups cooked chicken,
   cut into very small strips
1/2 cup thinly sliced radishes
1/2 cup sliced water chestnuts
2 Tbsp sliced scallions

1 In a large bowl, whisk the peanut butter, soy sauce, vinegar, and sesame oil until smooth. Stir in the ginger, garlic, and cayenne pepper.

2 Add the chicken, radishes, and water chestnuts. Toss lightly to mix. Top serving size portions with scallions.

Cucumber Salad

Serves 6

Serving size: 1/2 cup

Preparation time: 10 minutes

Exchanges
1/2 Carbohydrate

Calories 40
  Calories from Fat 2
Total Fat . . . . 0 g
  Saturated Fat . . . . 0 g
Cholesterol . . . . 0 mg
Sodium . . . . 3 mg
Carbohydrate . . . . 8 g
  Dietary Fiber . . . . 2 g
  Sugars . . . . 4 g
Protein . . . . 2 g

2 1/2 cups peeled, thinly sliced
       cucumbers
    1 medium onion, thinly sliced
  1/2 cup kidney beans (cooked)
    1 tsp Mrs. Dash
    1 tsp dill
  1/4 cup rice vinegar

1 Mix the cucumbers, onions, and beans together in a medium bowl. In a separate bowl, mix the remaining ingredients. Pour over the cucumbers and chill to serve.

Curried Tuna & Fruit Salad

Serves 4

Serving size: 1/4 recipe

Preparation time: 10 minutes

Exchanges
3 Very Lean Meat
1 1/2 Fruit

Calories	188
Calories from Fat	13
Total Fat	1 g
Saturated Fat	0 g
Cholesterol	24 mg
Sodium	288 mg
Carbohydrate	22 g
Dietary Fiber	3 g
Sugars	16 g
Protein	23 g

1/2 cup plain low-fat yogurt
2 tsp curry powder
1/4 tsp salt
1/4 tsp pepper
2 6-oz cans water-packed white tuna, drained
1 10-oz can mandarin oranges, drained
1 8-oz can sugar-free pineapple tidbits, drained
1/2 cup seedless green grapes, halved
1/2 cup seedless red grapes, halved
1/2 cup sliced water chestnuts, drained
4 cups romaine lettuce

1 In a large bowl, combine the yogurt, curry powder, salt, and pepper. Blend until smooth. Add the tuna, all the fruit, and water chestnuts.

2 Toss together gently until the fruits and tuna are coated with the dressing. Chill at least 4 hours.

3 Arrange the lettuce on 4 salad plates and top with the tuna and fruit mixture.

Egg Salad

Serves 4

Serving size: 1/4 recipe

Preparation time: 15 minutes

Exchanges
2 Medium-Fat Meat
1 Fat

Calories 184
   Calories from Fat 129
Total Fat . . . . 14 g
   Saturated Fat . . . . 4 g
Cholesterol . . . . 326 mg
Sodium . . . . 310 mg
Carbohydrate . . . . 3 g
   Dietary Fiber . . . . 0 g
   Sugars . . . . 1 g
Protein . . . . 10 g

6 eggs, boiled (15 minutes), peeled, and minced
1 stalk celery, chopped
1/4 cup minced onion
1/3 cup lite mayonnaise
1 Tbsp mustard
1/8 tsp black pepper

1 Combine all ingredients and chill before serving.

Jalapeño Tuna Salad

Serves 4

Serving size: 1/4 recipe

Preparation time: 10 minutes

Exchanges
2 Lean Meat
1/2 Fat

Calories............. 137
   Calories from Fat 61
Total Fat .... 7 g
   Saturated Fat.......... 2 g
Cholesterol.......... 122 mg
Sodium .... 554 mg
Carbohydrate.......... 4 g
   Dietary Fiber.......... 1 g
   Sugars .... 2 g
Protein .... 14 g

  1 6-oz can water-packed tuna
1/4 cup finely chopped onion
  1 celery stalk, chopped
  1 dill pickle, minced
1/8 tsp black pepper
  3 Tbsp lite mayonnaise
  2 hard-boiled eggs, chopped
  2 tsp mustard
  1 Tbsp minced jalapeño peppers

1 Combine all ingredients and chill before serving.

Marinated Italian Salad

Serves 8

Serving size: 1/8 recipe

Preparation time: 20 minutes

Exchanges
1 Vegetable
1 Fat

Calories	. . . .	72
Calories from Fat	. . . . .	37
Total Fat	. . . .	4 g
Saturated Fat	. . . .	1 g
Cholesterol	. . . .	0 mg
Sodium	. . . .	160 mg
Carbohydrate	. . . .	8 g
Dietary Fiber	. . . .	2 g
Sugars	. . . .	3 g
Protein	. . . .	3 g

1/4 cup low-sodium, low-fat chicken broth
2 Tbsp olive oil
2 Tbsp thinly sliced green onions
2 tsp Italian seasoning
2 tsp lemon juice
2 tsp cider vinegar
1/4 tsp salt (optional)
1/8 tsp black pepper
2–3 drops hot pepper sauce
4 cups small broccoli florets
1 cup water
1/2 cup sun-dried tomatoes, cut in quarters
2 Tbsp chopped black olives
1 jar (14 1/2 oz) water-packed artichoke hearts, drained
1 large red bell pepper, chopped

1 In a large bowl, whisk together the broth, oil, onion, Italian seasoning, lemon juice, vinegar, salt (if using), black pepper, and hot pepper sauce.

2 In a medium saucepan, combine the broccoli florets and water. Cover and bring to a boil over high heat. Add the sun-dried tomatoes. Reduce heat and simmer for 1–2 minutes, or until broccoli is bright green. Drain and rinse with cold running water.

3 Drain well and add to the bowl with the dressing. Add the black olives, artichokes, and red pepper. Toss to coat the vegetables well. Cover and marinate at room temperature for 10–30 minutes. Chill before serving.

Tuna Salad in Tomatoes

Serves 8

Serving size: 1/8 recipe

Preparation time: 20 minutes

Exchanges
1 Carbohydrate
3 Lean Meat

Calories.............. 261
   Calories from Fat 69
Total Fat .... 8 g
   Saturated Fat.......... 1 g
Cholesterol........... 76 mg
Sodium .... 1032 mg
Carbohydrate.......... 19 g
   Dietary Fiber.......... 3 g
   Sugars .... 11 g
Protein .... 28 g

1 can water-packed tuna, drained
1 hard-boiled egg, minced
1 celery stalk, minced
1/2 yellow onion, minced
1/4 cup lite mayonnaise
2 tsp mustard
1 small dill pickle, minced
4 large tomatoes, sliced 6 times
   from the navel
4 lettuce leaves
2 cups fat-free cottage cheese
2 Tbsp lite ranch dressing
1/8 tsp black pepper

1 Squeeze excess water from tuna. Mix the tuna, egg, celery, onion, mayonnaise, mustard, and pickle together.

2 Set a lettuce leaf on each plate and put 1/2 cup cottage cheese in the center of the leaf. Stuff each tomato with 1/2 cup of tuna salad.

3 Place each tomato on the cottage cheese and drizzle with 1/2 Tbsp dressing. Sprinkle with pepper to serve.

★ *Dressings & Sauces*

Cranberry Vinaigrette

Serves 4

Serving size: 1/4 recipe

Preparation time: 5 minutes

Exchanges
1/2 Carbohydrate

Calories 41
   Calories from Fat 1
Total Fat . . . . 0 g
   Saturated Fat. . . . . 0 g
Cholesterol. . . . . 0 mg
Sodium . . . . 25 mg
Carbohydrate. . . . . 10 g
   Dietary Fiber . . . . 0 g
   Sugars . . . . 10 g
Protein . . . . 0 g

  1 tsp powdered fruit pectin
1/4 tsp lemon-pepper seasoning
1/4 tsp poppy seeds
2/3 cup cranberry juice cocktail
  1 tsp white vinegar
1/2 tsp EQUAL® for Recipes **or**
1 1/2 packets EQUAL® sweetener **or**
  1 Tbsp EQUAL® Spoonful™

1 In a small bowl, stir together the pectin, lemon-pepper seasoning, and poppy seeds. Stir in the cranberry juice, vinegar, and Equal®.

2 Cover and chill at least 1 hour before serving. Store in refrigerator for up to 3 days in a jar with a tight-fitting lid.

Creamy Basil & Italian Herb Dressing

Serves 4

Serving size: 3 Tbsp

Preparation time: 5 minutes

Exchanges
Free Food

Calories	23
Calories from Fat	0
Total Fat	0 g
Saturated Fat	0 g
Cholesterol	1 mg
Sodium	125 mg
Carbohydrate	4 g
Dietary Fiber	0 g
Sugars	3 g
Protein	2 g

1/4 cup fat-free plain yogurt
1/4 cup fat-free mayonnaise
1/4 cup fat-free milk
1/2 tsp chopped fresh basil
1/4 tsp Italian seasoning
1/4 tsp garlic powder

1 Combine all ingredients in a small bowl and mix well. Store covered in the refrigerator for up to 1 week.

Creamy Blue Cheese Dressing

Serves 20

Serving size: 2 Tbsp

Preparation time: 5 minutes

Exchanges
1/2 Carbohydrate

Calories 30
   Calories from Fat 7
Total Fat . . . . 1 g
   Saturated Fat . . . . 1 g
Cholesterol . . . . 3 mg
Sodium . . . . 139 mg
Carbohydrate . . . . 4 g
   Dietary Fiber . . . . 0 g
   Sugars . . . . 2 g
Protein . . . . 1 g

1 cup fat-free mayonnaise
1 cup fat-free sour cream
2 oz blue cheese, crumbled
1 tsp garlic powder
3 Tbsp fat-free milk

1 Combine all ingredients in a small bowl and mix well. Chill for 1 hour before serving. Store covered in the refrigerator for up to 1 week.

Dilled Cucumber Dressing

Serves 8

Serving size: 2 Tbsp

Preparation time: 5 minutes

Exchanges
Free Food

Calories............... 23
   Calories from Fat 0
Total Fat .... 0 g
   Saturated Fat.......... 0 g
Cholesterol............. 1 mg
Sodium .... 53 mg
Carbohydrate........... 4 g
   Dietary Fiber.......... 0 g
   Sugars .... 2 g
Protein .... 1 g

1/2 cup fat-free sour cream
1/2 cup fat-free plain yogurt
1/2 cup cucumber, peeled, seeded,
     and finely chopped
1 1/2 Tbsp minced fresh chives
1 1/2 tsp Dijon mustard
1 1/2 tsp dill
   1 tsp cider vinegar

1 Combine all ingredients in a small bowl and mix well. Store covered in the refrigerator for up to 1 week.

Orange Vinaigrette

Serves 3

Serving size: 2 Tbsp

Preparation time: 5 minutes

Exchanges
1/2 Carbohydrate

Calories. 23
  Calories from Fat 2
Total Fat . . . . 0 g
  Saturated Fat. . . . . 0 g
Cholesterol. . . . . 0 mg
Sodium . . . . 120 mg
Carbohydrate. . . . . 5 g
  Dietary Fiber . . . . 0 g
  Sugars . . . . 5 g
Protein . . . . 1 g

1/4 cup orange juice
  1 Tbsp balsamic vinegar
  1 Tbsp Dijon mustard
1/8 tsp black pepper

1 Combine all ingredients in a small bowl and mix well. Chill to allow flavors to develop before serving. Store covered in the refrigerator for up to 1 week.

Perfect Meat Marinade

Serves 1

Serving size: whole recipe

Preparation time: 5 minutes

Exchanges
1 Carbohydrate

Calories	214
Calories from Fat	127
Total Fat	14 g
Saturated Fat.	0 g
Cholesterol.	0 mg
Sodium	196 mg
Carbohydrate.	10 g
Dietary Fiber	0 g
Sugars	10 g
Protein	1 g

2 Tbsp vegetable oil
1/2 cup dark rum
1/2 cup orange juice
2 Tbsp Worcestershire sauce

1 Combine all ingredients in a small bowl and mix well. Store covered in the refrigerator for up to 1 week.

(Please note that the nutrient analysis at left is somewhat misleading, since the marinade will not be eaten by itself but used to prepare several servings of meat. You can divide the values at left by the number of servings of meat to get a more accurate analysis for the marinade itself.)

Sage Chutney Dressing

Serves 8

Serving size: 2 Tbsp

Preparation time: 5 minutes

Exchanges
1/2 Carbohydrate

Calories. 28
   Calories from Fat 0
Total Fat . . . . 0 g
   Saturated Fat. . . . . 0 g
Cholesterol. . . . . 1 mg
Sodium . . . . 96 mg
Carbohydrate. . . . . 6 g
   Dietary Fiber . . . . 0 g
   Sugars . . . . 4 g
Protein . . . . 1 g

1/4 cup fat-free plain yogurt
1/4 cup fat-free sour cream
1/4 cup fat-free milk
1/2 Tbsp chopped chutney
1/4 tsp sage
1/4 tsp ginger
1/8 tsp salt

1 Combine all ingredients in a small bowl and mix well. Store covered in the refrigerator for up to 1 week.

Savory Balsamic Vinaigrette

Serves 8

Serving size: 2 Tbsp

Preparation time: 5 minutes

Exchanges
Free Food

Calories 13
   Calories from Fat 2
Total Fat . . . . 0 g
   Saturated Fat. . . . . 0 g
Cholesterol. . . . . 0 mg
Sodium . . . . 217 mg
Carbohydrate. . . . . 3 g
   Dietary Fiber . . . . 0 g
   Sugars . . . . 2 g
Protein . . . . 0 g

1/2 cup fat-free low-sodium chicken
    or vegetable broth
1/4 cup balsamic vinegar
  2 Tbsp catsup
  2 Tbsp mustard (prepared)
1/4 tsp savory
1/4 tsp thyme
1/8 tsp ground red pepper
1/2 tsp seasoning salt

1 Combine all ingredients in a small bowl and mix well. Chill for 1 hour before serving. Store covered in the refrigerator for up to 1 week.

Tomato Vinaigrette

Serves 4

Serving size: 1/4 recipe

Preparation time: 5 minutes

Exchanges
Free Food

Calories	6
Calories from Fat	1
Total Fat	0 g
Saturated Fat	0 g
Cholesterol	0 mg
Sodium	60 mg
Carbohydrate	1 g
Dietary Fiber	0 g
Sugars	1 g
Protein	0 g

1/2	cup tomatoes, peeled, seeded, and chopped
1	Tbsp white-wine vinegar
1/2	tsp basil
1/2	tsp thyme
1/2	tsp Dijon mustard
1/2	tsp lite soy sauce

1 In a blender, combine all ingredients and blend on medium to high speed until well combined, about 25 seconds. Store covered up to 2 days in the refrigerator. Shake well before serving.

★ Soups & Stews

Black-Eyed Pea Stew

Serves 12

Serving size: 1 bowl

Preparation time: 10 minutes

Exchanges
2 Starch
2 Very Lean Meat

Calories. 242
   Calories from Fat. 19
Total Fat . . . . 2 g
   Saturated Fat. . . . . 1 g
Cholesterol. . . . . 37 mg
Sodium . . . . 417 mg
Carbohydrate. . . . . 31 g
   Dietary Fiber . . . . 10 g
   Sugars . . . . 6 g
Protein . . . . 25 g

4 cups dried black-eyed peas
1 tsp black pepper
1 Tbsp seasoning salt
1 Tbsp chopped parsley
1 tsp onion powder
1/4 tsp garlic powder
1 1/2 lb lean ground turkey (or beef)
1 whole onion, chopped
2 tomatoes, minced
4 Tbsp sour cream

1 Fill a tall stockpot with 8 cups of water. Add all ingredients except the onion, meat, tomatoes, and sour cream. Cook for 4–6 hours over medium heat until the peas are tender.

2 Fry the meat and onion in a nonstick skillet until cooked. Add to the stew. Top each serving with some tomatoes and 1 tsp sour cream.

Mexican Vegetable Soup

Serves 8

Serving size: 1 cup

Preparation time: 15 minutes

Exchanges
1 Starch
2 Vegetable
1/2 Fat

Calories	155
Calories from Fat	33
Total Fat	4 g
Saturated Fat	1 g
Cholesterol	0 mg
Sodium	380 mg
Carbohydrate	24 g
Dietary Fiber	6 g
Sugars	9 g
Protein	8 g

2 Tbsp extra virgin olive oil
3–5 jalapeño peppers, stems and seeds removed
1 large onion, chopped
6 cups fat-free, reduced-sodium chicken broth
4 small carrots, thinly sliced
3/4 lb chayote squash, peeled and cut into 1/2-inch cubes
1 cup navy beans, cooked
1 cup okra, sliced and cooked
1 cup frozen corn
3/4 lb tomatoes (preferably plum), chopped
3/4 cup frozen peas
1 tsp cumin

1 Heat the oil in a large stockpot and sauté the onion and peppers until the onions are translucent, about 5 minutes.

2 Add the remaining ingredients and bring to a boil. Reduce to a simmer and cook, covered, for 15 minutes.

Old-Time Beef Stew

Serves 6

Serving size: 1 1/3 cups

Preparation time: 15 minutes

Exchanges
1/2 Starch
3 Very Lean Meat
3 Vegetable
1 Fat

Calories 261
   Calories from Fat 75
Total Fat . . . . 8 g
   Saturated Fat. . . . . 2 g
Cholesterol. . . . . 64 mg
Sodium . . . . 333 mg
Carbohydrate. . . . . 21 g
   Dietary Fiber. . . . . 4 g
   Sugars . . . . 12 g
Protein . . . . 25 g

1 1/2 lb boneless beef stew meat, cut into 1-inch cubes
1 Tbsp olive oil
4 cups water
1 large onion, chopped
2 cloves garlic, minced
2 Tbsp Worcestershire sauce
2 Tbsp orange juice
1/2 tsp salt
1/2 tsp paprika
1/8 tsp black pepper
1 bay leaf
1/8 tsp allspice
6 medium carrots, peeled and sliced into 3/4-inch chunks
1 lb small pearl onions
1 summer squash, chopped
1/2 cup cold water
1/4 cup all-purpose flour
6 Tbsp chopped parsley

1 Heat the oil in a large stockpot and cook the meat and the onion until the meat is browned on all sides.

2 Add the remaining ingredients except the cold water, flour, and parsley and simmer for 60 minutes. Discard the bay leaf.

3 In a covered jar, shake together the cold water and flour until combined. Stir into stew. Stir until stew is thickened and bubbly, about 5 minutes. Top each serving with 1 Tbsp parsley.

Pasta Vegetable Soup

Serves 8

Serving size: 1 cup

Preparation time: 10 minutes

Exchanges
1/2 Carbohydrate

Calories...............	58
Calories from Fat	8
Total Fat	1 g
Saturated Fat.........	0 g
Cholesterol.............	2 mg
Sodium	264 mg
Carbohydrate...........	8 g
Dietary Fiber..........	1 g
Sugars	2 g
Protein	4 g

1 medium carrot,
  peeled and thinly sliced
1 medium red bell pepper,
  seeded and cut into thin slices
1 quart water
1 quart fat-free, reduced-sodium
  chicken broth
1/2 tsp basil
1/2 tsp oregano
1/4 tsp thyme
1 cup packed fresh spinach,
  thinly sliced
1/4 lb fresh mushrooms, thinly sliced
2 oz dry angel hair pasta,
  broken into quarters
3 Tbsp grated Parmesan cheese

1 Combine all ingredients in a large stockpot except for the pasta and cheese and bring to a boil.

2 Add the pasta and cook for 5 minutes. Top each serving with Parmesan cheese.

Red Pepper Soup

Serves 8

Serving size: 1 cup

Preparation time: 25 minutes

Exchanges
1 Carbohydrate
1/2 Fat

Calories. 123
   Calories from Fat 31
Total Fat . . . . 3 g
   Saturated Fat. . . . . 1 g
Cholesterol. . . . . 0 mg
Sodium . . . . 364 mg
Carbohydrate. . . . . 17 g
   Dietary Fiber . . . . 3 g
   Sugars . . . . 10 g
Protein . . . . 7 g

2 Tbsp olive oil
2 cups chopped onions
2 cups thinly sliced red bell peppers
1/2 potato, peeled and grated
5 cups fat-free, reduced-sodium chicken broth
1 12-oz can evaporated fat-free milk
2 Tbsp fresh lime juice
2 Tbsp chopped fresh dill
8 sprigs fresh dill

1 Heat the oil in a large stockpot over medium heat and sauté the onions and red peppers for 15 minutes, stirring constantly.

2 Add the potato and broth. Cook an additional 15 minutes. Pureé in batches in the blender.

3 Combine the pureé and remaining ingredients except dill sprigs in the stockpot. Heat to serving temperature. Top each serving with a dill sprig.

Turkey Chili

Serves 4

Serving size: 1 cup

Preparation time: 20 minutes

Exchanges
1 1/2 Starch
4 Very Lean Meat
2 Vegetable

Calories	314
Calories from Fat	45
Total Fat	5 g
Saturated Fat	1 g
Cholesterol	70 mg
Sodium	98 mg
Carbohydrate	31 g
Dietary Fiber	9 g
Sugars	8 g
Protein	37 g

1 Tbsp olive oil
1 lb ground turkey (97% fat free)
1 onion, chopped
2 cloves garlic, minced
3 tomatoes, peeled and chopped
2 cups kidney beans, cooked
1/4 tsp molasses
1 1/2 Tbsp chili powder
1/8 tsp oregano
1/8 tsp cumin
1/4 tsp basil
1/4 tsp thyme
1 bay leaf

1 Heat the oil in a large stockpot over medium heat. Brown the meat, onion, and garlic until the meat is done.

2 Add the remaining ingredients and cook for at least 30 minutes or until thick. Discard the bay leaf.

3 You can top chili with additional chopped onions, tomatoes, green bell peppers, or low-fat cheddar cheese, or pour chili over rice or pasta.

Vegetable Shrimp Chowder

Serves 11
Serving size: 1 cup

Preparation time: 30 minutes

Exchanges
1 Starch
1 Very Lean Meat
1 Vegetable

Calories 134
   Calories from Fat 22
Total Fat . . . . 2 g
   Saturated Fat . . . . 0 g
Cholesterol . . . . 53 mg
Sodium . . . . 317 mg
Carbohydrate . . . . 20 g
   Dietary Fiber . . . . 3 g
   Sugars . . . . 5 g
Protein . . . . 10 g

4 1/2 cups frozen corn, thawed and divided
3 cups fat-free reduced-sodium chicken broth, divided
1 1/2 Tbsp olive oil
1 1/2 cups chopped onion
1 1/2 cups chopped green bell pepper
1 1/2 cups chopped red bell pepper
1 1/2 cups fat-free milk
1 lb medium shrimp, peeled
1/3 cup chopped fresh cilantro
1/3 cup chopped fresh parsley
1/3 tsp salt
1/4 tsp pepper
2 Tbsp lime juice
1/4 tsp Vege-Sal
1 tsp onion powder

1 Combine 3 1/2 cups corn and 2 cups broth in a blender. Cover and blend until smooth. Set aside.

2 Heat the oil in a large stockpot over medium heat. Add the onion and bell peppers and sauté for 5 minutes or until the vegetables are tender.

3 Stir in the puréed corn mixture, remaining 1 cup broth, and fat-free milk. Bring to a boil. Cover, reduce heat, and simmer for 5 minutes (be careful—the milk will curdle if the temperature gets too hot!).

4 Add the remaining 1 cup corn, shrimp, and the rest of the ingredients. Cover and simmer 5 minutes or until shrimp is done.

Vegetarian Chili

Serves 4

Serving size: 1 cup

Preparation time: 10 minutes

Exchanges
1 Starch
2 Vegetable
1 Fat

Calories	172
Calories from Fat	38
Total Fat	4 g
Saturated Fat	1 g
Cholesterol	0 mg
Sodium	361 mg
Carbohydrate	28 g
Dietary Fiber	8 g
Sugars	8 g
Protein	9 g

1 Tbsp olive oil
1 onion, chopped
2 cloves garlic, minced
1 Tbsp chili powder
1/8 tsp oregano
1/8 tsp cumin
1 bay leaf
2 8-oz cans chopped tomatoes with juice
1 5-oz can kidney beans, drained
1 cup chopped zucchini
1 chopped carrot
1 cup water

1 Heat the oil in a large stockpot over medium heat. Sauté the onion and garlic until soft. Add the remaining ingredients and cook for 30 minutes. Discard the bay leaf.

2 You can top chili with additional chopped onions, tomatoes, green bell peppers, or low-fat cheddar cheese, or pour chili over rice or pasta.

★ *Veggies & Side Dishes*

Asparagus in Parmesan Cheese Sauce

Serves 4

Serving size: 1/4 recipe

Preparation time: 5 minutes

Exchanges
1 Medium-Fat Meat
1 Vegetable

Calories................89
   Calories from Fat.....53
Total Fat...............6 g
   Saturated Fat..........4 g
Cholesterol...........17 mg
Sodium...............336 mg
Carbohydrate..........5 g
   Dietary Fiber..........1 g
   Sugars...............2 g
Protein................5 g

1 lb fresh asparagus
1 Tbsp butter
1 Tbsp flour
1/4 cup fat-free reduced-sodium chicken broth
1/4 cup fat-free milk
2 Tbsp low-fat cheddar cheese, shredded
3 Tbsp Parmesan cheese, grated
1/4 tsp salt
1/4 tsp pepper

1 Wash asparagus under cool running water. Cut away ends of asparagus and blanch in boiling water until cooked, but firm. Drain and keep warm.

2 Melt the butter in a small skillet and whisk in the flour. Add the broth and milk gradually. Cook, stirring, until mixture thickens.

3 Stir in the cheeses and seasonings. Pour the cheese sauce over the asparagus and serve.

Broccoli-Cauliflower Au Gratin

Serves 4

Serving size: 1 cup

Preparation time: 15 minutes

Exchanges
1/2 Starch
1 Vegetable
1/2 Fat

Calories	88
Calories from Fat	32
Total Fat	4 g
Saturated Fat	2 g
Cholesterol	9 mg
Sodium	232 mg
Carbohydrate	11 g
Dietary Fiber	2 g
Sugars	3 g
Protein	4 g

2 cups small broccoli florets, steamed
2 cups small cauliflower florets, steamed
1/3 cup dry breadcrumbs
2 Tbsp sharp low-fat cheddar cheese
1 Tbsp melted butter
1 Tbsp mustard
1/8 tsp white pepper

1 Heat the oven to 425°F. Spray a 1 1/2-qt casserole dish with nonstick cooking spray and place the vegetables in the dish.

2 Sprinkle all ingredients over vegetables and bake for 10 minutes.

Broccoli Cheese Casserole

Serves 6

Serving size: 1/6 recipe

Preparation time: 15 minutes

Exchanges
1 Carbohydrate
1 Fat

Calories. 126
   Calories from Fat 43
Total Fat . . . . 5 g
   Saturated Fat. . . . . 2 g
Cholesterol. . . . . 12 mg
Sodium . . . . .356 mg
Carbohydrate. . . . . 16 g
   Dietary Fiber. . . . . 3 g
   Sugars . . . . 4 g
Protein . . . . 6 g

1/2 cup dry breadcrumbs
1 tsp garlic powder
1 tsp herb seasoning
4 cups broccoli spears, blanched
1 10 3/4-oz can reduced-fat cream of chicken soup
2 tsp lemon juice
1 Tbsp melted butter
1/4 cup low-fat shredded cheddar cheese

1 Heat the oven to 350°F. Sprinkle the breadcrumbs with the garlic powder and herb seasoning. Mix well and set aside.

2 Arrange the broccoli evenly in an 8 × 8 baking pan. In a medium bowl, whisk together the soup and lemon juice. Pour over the broccoli.

3 Add butter to the breadcrumbs and stir. Sprinkle on top of the broccoli and bake for 30 minutes or until heated thoroughly. Sprinkle with cheddar cheese. Serve warm.

Cheesy Spinach-Stuffed Potatoes

Serves 4

Serving size: 1 stuffer

Preparation time: 30 minutes

Exchanges
2 Starch
1 Vegetable
1/2 Fat

Calories 221	
Calories from Fat 44	
Total Fat . . . . 5 g	
Saturated Fat . . . . 2 g	
Cholesterol . . . . 8 mg	
Sodium . . . . 315 mg	
Carbohydrate . . . . 35 mg	
Dietary Fiber . . . . 5 g	
Sugars . . . . 6 g	
Protein . . . . 12 g	

2 russet potatoes, baked and cooled
2 tsp olive oil
1 small onion, chopped
1 clove garlic, minced
1 tsp basil
1 tsp tarragon
1 tsp marjoram
2 carrots, diced
12 oz frozen spinach, thawed, pressed dry, and minced
3 Tbsp Parmesan cheese
1/4 cup shredded low-fat cheddar cheese
1/2 cup low-fat cottage cheese

1 Heat the oven to 350°F. Heat the oil in a large skillet and sauté all ingredients except the cheeses for 5 minutes.

2 Cut the potatoes in half and hollow out the pulps, leaving the skins intact. Mix the potato pulp with the cheeses. Stir in the vegetable mixture and stuff each potato shell.

3 Bake 20 minutes and serve.

Crockpot Baked Beans

Serves 10

Serving size: 1/2 cup

Preparation time: 10 minutes

Exchanges
1 1/2 Starch
1 Very Lean Meat

Calories 155
   Calories from Fat 20
Total Fat . . . . 2 g
   Saturated Fat. . . . . 0 g
Cholesterol . . . . 13 mg
Sodium . . . . 637 mg
Carbohydrate . . . . 26 g
   Dietary Fiber . . . . 6 g
   Sugars . . . . 9 g
Protein . . . . 11 g

1/2 medium onion, chopped
  6 slices turkey bacon, chopped
  4 oz lean ground beef
  1 24-oz can vegetarian baked beans
  1 12-oz can tomato sauce
  1 16-oz can red kidney beans, rinsed and drained
  2 Tbsp molasses
  1 tsp liquid smoke
1/2 tsp maple extract

1 Cook the onion, bacon, and beef over medium-high heat for 10 minutes. Transfer the mixture to a crockpot.

2 Add the remaining ingredients and stir well. Cook on medium for 4 hours, stirring occasionally.

Dilled Brussels Sprouts in Cream Sauce

Serves 4

Serving size: 1/4 recipe

Preparation time: 20 minutes

Exchanges
2 Vegetable
1/2 Fat

Calories..............	77
Calories from Fat	19
Total Fat	2 g
Saturated Fat.........	1 g
Cholesterol............	6 mg
Sodium	67 mg
Carbohydrate..........	13 g
Dietary Fiber..........	3 g
Sugars	6 g
Protein	4 g

1/2 cup fat-free milk
1 Tbsp cornstarch
1 tsp minced fresh dill
1/8 tsp garlic powder
1/8 tsp black pepper
1 oz light cream cheese, cubed
10 cherry tomatoes, halved
12 oz fresh cooked Brussels sprouts
(reserve 1/4 cup cooking liquid)

1 Combine the milk, cornstarch, dill, garlic powder, pepper, and reserved cooking liquid in a medium saucepot and cook over medium heat, stirring, until mixture thickens and comes to a gentle boil.

2 Stir in the cream cheese and cook until it melts. Add the Brussels sprouts and tomatoes and gently stir until heated.

Garlic-Sautéed Spinach & Onions

Serves 3

Serving size: 1/3 cup

Preparation time: 10 minutes

Exchanges
1 Vegetable
1 Fat

Calories	62
Calories from Fat	37
Total Fat	4 g
Saturated Fat	2 g
Cholesterol	5 mg
Sodium	534 mg
Carbohydrate	5 g
Dietary Fiber	2 g
Sugars	3 g
Protein	2 g

1 1/2	tsp olive oil
1 1/2	tsp butter
5	cups fresh chopped spinach leaves
1	onion, chopped
1/4	tsp garlic powder
1	tsp Vege-Sal

1 Heat the olive oil and butter over medium-high heat and sauté all ingredients until spinach is limp and tender. Serve hot.

Grilled Summer Vegetables

Serves 4

Serving size: 1 packet

Preparation time: 20 minutes

Exchanges
2 Vegetable
1/2 Fat

Calories 82
   Calories from Fat 32
Total Fat . . . . 4 g
   Saturated Fat . . . . 1 g
Cholesterol . . . . 0 mg
Sodium . . . . 386 mg
Carbohydrate . . . . 12 g
   Dietary Fiber . . . . 4 g
   Sugars . . . . 7 g
Protein . . . . 3 g

1/2 medium size eggplant,
    cut into cubes
  2 medium zucchini squash,
    cut into cubes
  1 medium summer squash,
    cut into cubes
  1 medium sweet red pepper,
    seeded and cut into thin strips
  1 medium vidalia onion,
    thinly sliced
  1 Tbsp olive oil
  2 tsp chopped fresh dill
1/8 tsp pepper
  1 tsp seasoning salt

1 Toss the vegetables with the olive oil until coated. Arrange equal amounts of vegetables on 4 12-inch squares of aluminum foil. Sprinkle each square with equal amounts of seasonings.

2 Fold foil over vegetables, sealing securely. Grill 6 inches above medium-hot coals for 15 minutes, turning once.

Macaroni & Cheese

Serves 8

Serving size: 1/2 cup

Preparation time: 15 minutes

Exchanges
2 Starch

Calories. 154
   Calories from Fat 9
Total Fat . . . . 1 g
   Saturated Fat. . . . . 0 g
Cholesterol. . . . . 3 mg
Sodium . . . . 143 mg
Carbohydrate . . . . 27 g
   Dietary Fiber. . . . . 1 g
   Sugars . . . . 4 g
Protein . . . . 8 g

1 1/2	Tbsp cornstarch
1 1/2	cups fat-free milk
1/2	cup low-fat shredded sharp cheddar cheese
1/4	cup fat-free cottage cheese
1/2	cup onion, finely minced
1	tsp dry mustard
1/2	tsp Mrs. Dash
1/8	tsp pepper
	Hot pepper sauce to taste (optional)
8	oz macaroni, cooked and drained
2	Tbsp seasoned breadcrumbs

1 Heat the oven to 350°F. Mix the cornstarch and milk in a saucepan; bring to a low boil. Reduce heat, stirring constantly with a wire whisk, until slightly thickened. Remove from heat.

2 Add all ingredients to milk mixture except breadcrumbs; mix well. Spray an 8 × 8 baking pan with nonstick cooking spray.

3 Pour the mixture into the pan and bake for 25 minutes.

Oven-Roasted Asparagus

Serves 4

Serving size: 1/4 recipe

Preparation time: 10 minutes

Exchanges
1 Vegetable

Calories	24
Calories from Fat	11
Total Fat	1 g
Saturated Fat	0 g
Cholesterol	0 mg
Sodium	152 mg
Carbohydrate	3 g
Dietary Fiber	1 g
Sugars	1 g
Protein	1 g

1 lb new asparagus
   (narrow, tender stalks)
2 cloves garlic, slivered
2 Tbsp water
2 Tbsp nonalcoholic white wine
2 tsp lemon juice
1 tsp olive oil
1/4 tsp salt
1/8 tsp black pepper

1 Heat the oven to 400°F. Scatter the garlic in a 13 × 9 baking dish. Arrange the asparagus in a single layer.

2 In a small bowl, combine the water, wine, lemon juice, oil, salt, and pepper. Pour over the asparagus. Bake at 400°F for 8–10 minutes.

3 Turn asparagus over and roast for an additional 8–10 minutes or until the asparagus is tender but still firm. The liquid should almost be gone from the baking dish.

Ratatouille in Roasted Peppers

Serves 4

Serving size: 2 pepper shells

Preparation time: 60 minutes

Exchanges
1 Carbohydrate
1 Vegetable

Calories. 99
   Calories from Fat 13
Total Fat . . . . 1 g
   Saturated Fat. . . . . 0 g
Cholesterol. . . . . 4 mg
Sodium . . . . 63 mg
Carbohydrate. . . . . 19 g
   Dietary Fiber . . . . 5 g
   Sugars . . . . 6 g
Protein . . . . 5 g

4 red, green, or yellow bell peppers
2 cups eggplant, diced
1 medium zucchini, chopped into chunks
1 cup sliced fresh mushrooms
1 8-oz can stewed tomatoes with juice
1/2 cup chopped onions
1/4 cup minced fresh basil
2 Tbsp dry white wine
2 cloves garlic, minced
1/4 cup reduced-fat mozzarella cheese, finely shredded

1 Preheat the oven to 450°F. Cut peppers in half lengthwise. Remove stems, seeds, and membranes. Arrange pepper halves cut side down on a nonstick baking sheet. Spray skins of peppers with nonstick cooking spray. Bake for 25–35 minutes or until skins just begin to blister.

2 Remove peppers from the oven and cool slightly. When the peppers are cool enough to handle, remove and discard the skins. Return the peppers, cut side up, to the baking sheet and set aside.

3 Preheat the broiler. Combine all remaining ingredients except the cheese in a large skillet and bring to a boil. Reduce heat, cover, and simmer for about 20 minutes or until the vegetables are tender. Uncover and simmer for 5–10 minutes more, stirring occasionally, until mixture thickens slightly.

4 Spoon the ratatouille mixture into the pepper shells. Sprinkle with cheese. Broil 3–4 inches from the heat for 1 minute or until the cheese melts.

Risotto with Asparagus & Apples

Serves 4

Serving size: 1 cup

Preparation time: 45 minutes

Exchanges
2 Starch

Calories 151	
Calories from Fat 17	
Total Fat . . . . 2 g	
Saturated Fat . . . . 1 g	
Cholesterol . . . . 2 mg	
Sodium . . . . 195 mg	
Carbohydrate . . . . 29 g	
Dietary Fiber . . . . 2 g	
Sugars . . . . 4 g	
Protein . . . . 4 g	

3 1/4 cups water
 3/4 cup fat-free reduced-sodium
        chicken broth
   8 oz fresh asparagus spears,
        trimmed and cut diagonally
        into 1-inch pieces
 1/2 cup grated apples
   1 tsp extra-virgin olive oil
 3/4 cup Arborio rice
   1 Tbsp Parmesan cheese
   1 Tbsp chopped parsley
 1/8 tsp salt
 1/8 tsp black pepper

1 Bring the water and broth to boil in a medium saucepan. Add the asparagus, return to a boil, and cook uncovered for 2–3 minutes. Stir in the apples, then remove the asparagus and apples from the liquid with a strainer. Cool the vegetables under cold running water and set aside.

2 Reduce the heat under the broth mixture so it simmers. Heat the oil over medium heat in a skillet and brown the rice for 2–3 minutes or until the rice turns golden. Add a large ladle of the broth mixture to rice and bring to a boil. Cook, stirring frequently, for 1–3 minutes or until liquid is nearly absorbed.

3 Repeat the process with the remaining broth mixture, adding a ladle at a time until rice is creamy and al dente, and the liquid is nearly absorbed. This process will take about 30 minutes.

4 Stir the asparagus and apples into rice. Cook for 1–2 minutes or until heated thoroughly. Remove pan from heat and stir in the Parmesan cheese, parsley, salt, and pepper.

Santa Fe Stuffed Chiles

Serves 2

Serving size: 3 chile halves

Preparation time: 10 minutes

Exchanges
3 Carbohydrate
1 Medium-Fat Meat
1 Fat

Calories. 347
   Calories from Fat 133
Total Fat . . . . 15 g
   Saturated Fat. . . . . 5 g
Cholesterol . . . . 21 mg
Sodium . . . . 755 mg
Carbohydrate . . . . 43 g
   Dietary Fiber . . . . 4 g
   Sugars . . . . 20 g
Protein . . . . 18 g

3 fresh poblano chiles
1/2 cup corn
1/2 cup finely chopped red onion
1/3 cup Parmesan cheese
1/3 cup finely chopped plum
   tomatoes
1/4 cup dry breadcrumbs
1/4 cup chopped fresh cilantro
2 Tbsp plain fat-free yogurt
2 Tbsp low-fat mayonnaise
1 tsp chili powder
1/4 tsp black pepper
1 Tbsp olive oil
6 Tbsp plain fat-free yogurt

1 Preheat oven to 375°F. Cut chiles in half lengthwise, discarding seeds and membranes.

2 Combine all ingredients except yogurt in a bowl. Stuff chile halves evenly with vegetable mixture. Place stuffed chiles on a nonstick baking sheet and bake for 20 minutes.

3 Top each chile half with 1 Tbsp yogurt and serve.

Banana-Strawberry Smoothie
page 72

PHOTOGRAPHS BY TARAN Z; FOOD PREPARATION AND STYLING BY SUSAN BOND FORESMAN

Asparagus in Parmesan Cheese Sauce
page 110

Crispy Oven-Fried Chicken
page 134

Crab Cakes with Yogurt Tartar Sauce
page 142

Marinated Beef Kabobs
page 154

Blueberry Almond Muffins
page 162

Chocolate Almond Mousse
page 174

Apple Crisp
page 170

Sautéed Okra

Serves 4

Serving size: 1 cup

Preparation time: 5 minutes

Exchanges
2 Vegetable
1 Fat

Calories. 103
   Calories from Fat 56
Total Fat . . . . 6 g
   Saturated Fat. . . . . 1 g
Cholesterol. . . . . 0 mg
Sodium . . . . 288 mg
Carbohydrate. . . . . 10 g
   Dietary Fiber . . . . 3 g
   Sugars . . . . 4 g
Protein . . . . 2 g

4 cups fresh okra
2 Tbsp olive oil
1 tsp Italian herbs
1/2 tsp seasoning salt
1/4 tsp Vege-Sal
1 onion, chopped

1 Heat the oil over medium heat. Add all ingredients and cook, covered, until okra is tender.

Scalloped Potatoes

Serves 6

Serving size: 1/6 recipe

Preparation time: 20 minutes

Exchanges
2 1/2 Starch

Calories	188
Calories from Fat	39
Total Fat	4 g
Saturated Fat	1 g
Cholesterol	0 mg
Sodium	19 mg
Carbohydrate	35 g
Dietary Fiber	3 g
Sugars	6 g
Protein	4 g

2 Tbsp olive oil
2 large white onions, thinly sliced
2 bay leaves
1/2 tsp thyme
1/8 tsp garlic powder
1/2 cup fat-free milk
2 1/4 lb potatoes, very thinly sliced

1 Preheat the oven to 400°F. Heat the oil over medium heat in a large skillet and sauté the onions for 5 minutes.

2 Add the seasonings and milk. Stir and heat to a simmer. Remove from heat. Spray a 2-qt casserole dish with nonstick cooking spray.

3 Place the potatoes in the dish and pour the onion mixture over the potatoes. Bake for 1 hour or until potatoes are tender.

Turkey Bacon Cabbage

Serves 6

Serving size: 1/2 cup

Preparation time: 10 minutes

Exchanges
2 Vegetable
1 Fat

Calories	97
Calories from Fat	50
Total Fat	6 g
Saturated Fat	1 g
Cholesterol	5 mg
Sodium	362 mg
Carbohydrate	11 g
Dietary Fiber	4 g
Sugars	6 g
Protein	4 g

2 Tbsp olive oil
1 cabbage, chopped
1/2 green bell pepper, chopped
1/2 red bell pepper, chopped
1/2 yellow bell pepper, chopped
1 large onion, chopped
3 strips turkey bacon, cooked, drained, and crumbled
1/2 tsp pepper
1 tsp seasoning salt
1 tsp garlic herb seasoning

1 Heat the oil in a stockpot over low heat. Add all ingredients and stir.

2 Cook, covered, until the cabbage is tender (about 20 minutes), stirring occasionally.

Vegetable Medley

Serves 6

Serving size: 1/6 recipe

Preparation time: 10 minutes

Exchanges
2 Vegetable
1 Fat

Calories. 94
   Calories from Fat 40
Total Fat . . . . 4 g
   Saturated Fat. . . . . 1 g
Cholesterol. . . . . 0 mg
Sodium . . . . 504 mg
Carbohydrate. . . . . 12 g
   Dietary Fiber . . . . 5 g
   Sugars . . . . 6 g
Protein . . . . 3 g

  2 Tbsp olive oil
  2 medium zucchini, sliced
  2 medium yellow squash, sliced
  1 whole onion, sliced
1/2 red bell pepper, sliced
1/2 yellow bell pepper, sliced
1/2 green bell pepper, sliced
  1 broccoli stalk, sliced
  2 cups okra, sliced
  1 Tbsp garlic herb seasoning
  1 tsp seasoning salt
  1 tsp pepper
  1 tsp Vege-Sal

1 Heat the oil in a stockpot and add all ingredients. Stir well and cook over medium heat for 10 minutes. Stir occasionally.

★ Chicken & Turkey

Balsamic Turkey & Peppers

Serves 4

Serving size: 1/4 recipe

Preparation time: 15 minutes

Exchanges
3 Lean Meat
2 Vegetable

Calories 225
   Calories from Fat 78
Total Fat . . . . 9 g
   Saturated Fat . . . . 1 g
Cholesterol . . . . 69 mg
Sodium . . . . 446 mg
Carbohydrate . . . . 9 g
   Dietary Fiber . . . . 2 g
   Sugars . . . . 3 g
Protein . . . . 28 g

2 Tbsp whole-wheat flour
1 tsp seasoning salt
1/8 tsp black pepper
4 4-oz turkey breast cutlets
1 Tbsp plus 1 tsp olive oil
1 large green bell pepper, sliced
1 large red bell pepper, sliced
3 cloves garlic, minced
1 tsp dried basil
   (or 1/4 cup chopped fresh)
2 Tbsp balsamic vinegar

1 Combine the flour, salt, and pepper on a plate and press the turkey cutlets into the mixture, coating them evenly on both sides and shaking off excess.

2 In a heavy 12-inch skillet over medium-high heat, heat 1 Tbsp olive oil. Add the turkey and brown for 2 minutes on each side. Transfer the cutlets to a platter and keep warm.

3 Add the remaining tsp of olive oil to the skillet along with the peppers and garlic. Reduce the heat to low, cover, and cook for 3–5 minutes, stirring occasionally, until peppers are tender-crisp.

4 Add the basil and vinegar to the skillet along with the turkey cutlets. Raise the heat to medium and cook an additional 2 minutes, stirring.

Broiled Rosemary Chicken

Serves 4

Serving size: 1 breast half

Preparation time: 5 minutes

Exchanges
4 Lean Meat

Calories. 224
   Calories from Fat 87
Total Fat . . . . 10 g
   Saturated Fat. . . . . 2 g
Cholesterol. . . . . 86 mg
Sodium . . . . 76 mg
Carbohydrate. . . . . 0 g
   Dietary Fiber. . . . . 0 g
   Sugars . . . . 0 g
Protein . . . . 32 g

  2 Tbsp white wine vinegar
  2 Tbsp extra virgin olive oil
  1 tsp minced fresh rosemary
  1 tsp minced fresh thyme
1/2 tsp tarragon
  1 tsp onion powder
1/8 tsp black pepper
  4 boneless, skinless chicken breast
    halves (5 oz each)

1 Combine all ingredients in a shallow dish except the chicken. Add the chicken, turning to coat, and marinate covered in the refrigerator for 30 minutes.

2 Heat the oven to broil and broil the chicken for 15 minutes on each side.

Easy Chicken Fettucine

Serves 6

Serving size: 1/6 recipe

Preparation time: 15 minutes

Exchanges
2 1/2 Starch
2 Lean Meat

Calories.............300
   Calories from Fat.....60
Total Fat.............6 g
   Saturated Fat.........1 g
Cholesterol...........40 mg
Sodium.............340 mg
Carbohydrate.........38 g
   Dietary Fiber.........2 g
   Sugars..............4 g
Protein..............21 g

8 oz plain or spinach fettucine
2 boneless, skinless chicken breast
  halves, cut into chunks
1/2 cup fat-free milk
1/4 cup reduced-calorie margarine
3/4 tsp garlic powder
1/4 tsp pepper
3/4 cup fat-free Parmesan cheese

1 Cook the fettucine as directed on the package; drain. Meanwhile, cook the chicken in a nonstick skillet until done.

2 Add milk and margarine to the hot fettucine. Stir in the chicken, seasonings, and cheese.

Fiery Chicken Fajitas

Serves 4

Serving size: 1 fajita

Preparation time: 30 minutes

Exchanges
1 Starch
3 Very Lean Meat
1 Vegetable
1/2 Fat

Calories. 227
   Calories from Fat 42
Total Fat . . . . 5 g
   Saturated Fat. . . . . 1 g
Cholesterol. . . . . 68 mg
Sodium . . . . 253 mg
Carbohydrate. . . . . 18 g
   Dietary Fiber . . . . 3 g
   Sugars . . . . 3 g
Protein . . . . 27 g

1 lb boneless, skinless chicken breast, sliced diagonally
2 Tbsp lemon or lime juice
1 Tbsp rice vinegar
1 Tbsp Worcestershire sauce
1/8 tsp salt
1/8 tsp pepper
1/4 tsp cumin
1 tsp extra virgin olive oil
2 cloves garlic, minced
1/4 green bell pepper, chopped
1/4 onion, chopped
1/4 tomato, chopped
1 cup pickled carrots
4 corn tortillas, warmed
8 Tbsp salsa

1 Place the chicken in a shallow dish. Combine the lemon juice and next 6 ingredients, stirring well. Pour over chicken, cover, and marinate in refrigerator for 30 minutes to 1 hour. Remove chicken from marinade.

2 Heat the oil over medium-high heat in a large skillet. Sauté the garlic, chicken, peppers, and onion for 5 minutes. Add the tomatoes and carrots and sauté for 2 more minutes or until the chicken is done.

3 Divide the ingredients between 4 tortillas. Top each with 2 Tbsp salsa and serve.

Chicken Sage Rampage

Serves 4

Serving size: 1/4 recipe

Preparation time: 15 minutes

Exchanges
2 Starch
4 Very Lean Meat

Calories. 289
  Calories from Fat 42
Total Fat . . . . 5 g
  Saturated Fat. . . . . 1 g
Cholesterol. . . . . 71 mg
Sodium . . . . 303 mg
Carbohydrate . . . . 29 g
  Dietary Fiber . . . . 2 g
  Sugars . . . . 5 g
Protein . . . . 30 g

1/2 cup fat-free plain yogurt
1/2 cup fat-free mayonnaise
  3 Tbsp finely chopped onions
1/2 tsp ginger
1/2 tsp sage
  1 lb boneless, skinless chicken
    breast, chopped into chunks
  1 tsp paprika
1/2 tsp black pepper
  2 cups cooked brown rice

1 In a small bowl, stir together the yogurt, mayonnaise, onions, ginger, and sage; set aside. Place the chicken in a medium bowl. Sprinkle with paprika and pepper and toss to coat.

2 Cook the chicken over medium-high heat in a large nonstick skillet for 5 minutes or until the chicken is done. Stir in the yogurt mixture and cook for 2 more minutes. Serve over hot rice.

Chinese Chicken Stir-Fry

Serves 2

Serving size: 1/2 recipe

Preparation time: 10 minutes

Exchanges
1/2 Starch
3 Lean Meat
2 Vegetable
1/2 Fat

Calories.	293
Calories from Fat	90
Total Fat	10 g
Saturated Fat.	2 g
Cholesterol.	72 mg
Sodium	828 mg
Carbohydrate.	19 g
Dietary Fiber.	4 g
Sugars	9 g
Protein	32 g

1   Tbsp peanut oil
1   clove garlic, finely chopped
6   oz boneless, skinless chicken
    breast, cut into strips
1/2 lb Chinese pea pods
    (about 2 1/2 cups), washed
    and trimmed
1/3 cup chicken broth
2   Tbsp rice vinegar
2   Tbsp lite soy sauce
1   tsp oyster sauce
2   oz bean sprouts (about 1 cup)
1   Tbsp cornstarch
2   Tbsp cold water
1/2 cup canned baby corn
    Mandarin orange slices for
    garnish

1 Heat the peanut oil over high heat in a large wok or skillet. Add the garlic, chicken, and pea pods and stir-fry for 5 minutes.

2 Add the broth, vinegar, and soy sauce. Mix the cornstarch with the water and add to wok. Add the baby corn and stir-fry until the sauce is thickened and bubbly. Serve garnished with Mandarin orange slices.

Crispy Oven-Fried Chicken

Serves 6

Serving size: 1 breast half

Preparation time: 10 minutes

Exchanges
1 Starch
4 Very Lean Meat

Calories. 204
   Calories from Fat 37
Total Fat . . . . 4 g
   Saturated Fat. . . . . 1 g
Cholesterol. . . . . 108 mg
Sodium . . . . 155 mg
Carbohydrate. . . . . 11 g
   Dietary Fiber . . . . 2 g
   Sugars . . . . 1 g
Protein . . . . 30 g

  6 boneless, skinless chicken breast halves
1/3 cup whole-wheat flour
  2 eggs, lightly beaten (1 whole egg, 1 white)
  1 cup bran flake crumbs
1/4 tsp garlic powder
1/4 tsp pepper
1/4 tsp seasoning salt (optional)

1 Preheat the oven to 375°F. Combine the flour and seasonings in a bowl. Dip each piece of chicken in the flour mixture and coat evenly, then dip the chicken in the egg and roll in the bran crumbs.

2 Place the coated chicken pieces on a nonstick baking sheet. Bake 20–30 minutes until chicken is tender and no longer pink. Do not turn chicken over during baking.

Grilled Dijon Chicken Breasts

Serves 4

Serving size: 1 breast half

Preparation time: 10 minutes

Exchanges
1/2 Carbohydrate
4 Very Lean Meat

Calories 186
    Calories from Fat 29
Total Fat . . . . 3 g
    Saturated Fat . . . . 1 g
Cholesterol . . . . 68 mg
Sodium . . . . 245 mg
Carbohydrate . . . . 9 g
    Dietary Fiber . . . . 0 g
    Sugars . . . . 8 g
Protein . . . . 26 g

    4 boneless, skinless chicken breast
       halves
    1 cup dry white wine
  1/2 cup finely diced onions
    2 tsp dried whole tarragon leaves
    2 Tbsp Dijon mustard
    2 Tbsp molasses
  1/8 tsp pepper
  1/8 tsp salt (optional)

1 Heat the oven to broil. In a small saucepan, reduce the white wine, onions, and tarragon until half the liquid is left. Remove from heat and stir in the mustard, molasses, pepper, and salt. Set aside half of the sauce.

2 Coat the chicken with half the molasses-mustard sauce and broil (or grill) for 5–8 minutes on each side or until done. Serve with extra sauce on the side.

Low-Fat Turkey & Cheese Enchiladas

Serves 6

Serving size: 1 enchilada

Preparation time: 30 minutes

Exchanges
2 Starch
2 Very Lean Meat
1 Vegetable
1/2 Fat

Calories............. 266
  Calories from Fat 63
Total Fat .... 7 g
  Saturated Fat......... 3 g
Cholesterol........... 41 mg
Sodium .... 417 mg
Carbohydrate .... 32 g
  Dietary Fiber.......... 7 g
  Sugars .... 7 g
Protein .... 21 g

1 tsp olive oil
1/2 lb fresh ground turkey meat (97% fat-free), cooked
1 red bell pepper, chopped
1 onion, chopped
1 clove garlic, minced
1/2 cup sliced mushrooms
1/2 cup sliced zucchini
1 1/2 cups cooked pinto beans
1 1/2 cups chopped tomatoes
1 Tbsp chili powder
1 tsp cumin
1/4 tsp coriander
1/2 tsp seasoning salt
1/4 tsp black pepper
1/2 cup fat-free ricotta cheese
1/4 cup fat-free plain yogurt
6 corn tortillas
1/2 cup shredded low-fat cheddar cheese

1 Heat the oil over medium-high heat in a large skillet and sauté the meat, peppers, onion, garlic, mushrooms, and zucchini for 5–7 minutes or until the meat is cooked. Add the beans, tomatoes, and seasonings. Remove from heat.

2 Heat the oven to 350°F. Mix the ricotta and yogurt together in a small bowl. Soften the tortillas by steaming in the microwave for 20 seconds on high power.

3 Place 4 tsp cheese and 2 Tbsp yogurt mixture on each tortilla. Roll up and place in a nonstick baking dish. Top enchiladas with the meat mixture. Bake for 15–20 minutes.

Turkey Meatloaf

Serves 4

Serving size: 1/4 recipe

Preparation time: 15 minutes

Exchanges
1 Starch
4 Very Lean Meat
1 Fat

Calories 261
   Calories from Fat 79
Total Fat . . . . 9 g
   Saturated Fat. . . . . 2 g
Cholesterol. . . . . 123 mg
Sodium . . . . 536 mg
Carbohydrate. . . . . 10 g
   Dietary Fiber . . . . 2 g
   Sugars . . . . 3 g
Protein . . . . 33 g

1 lb lean ground turkey
   (97% fat-free)
1 egg and 2 egg whites
1 medium onion, minced
1/2 cup quick-cooking dry oatmeal
1 tsp Italian seasoning
3/4 tsp salt
3/4 tsp garlic powder
1/8 tsp pepper
2 Tbsp olive oil

1 Heat the oven to 350°F. Combine all ingredients except olive oil in a large bowl and form into a loaf.

2 Place the loaf on a rack in a roasting pan and brush loaf with olive oil. Bake for 1 1/4 hours.

★ *Seafood*

Baked Citrus Halibut

Serves 4

Serving size: 1 steak

Preparation time: 10 minutes

Exchanges
4 Very Lean Meat

Calories 140
   Calories from Fat 22
Total Fat . . . . 2 g
   Saturated Fat . . . . 0 g
Cholesterol . . . . 36 mg
Sodium . . . . 63 mg
Carbohydrate . . . . 4 g
   Dietary Fiber . . . . 0 g
   Sugars . . . . 3 g
Protein . . . . 24 g

4 4-oz halibut steaks,
    cut 3/4 inch thick
1/3 cup finely chopped onions
2 cloves garlic, minced
2 Tbsp chopped fresh parsley
1/2 tsp finely grated lemon peel
1/2 tsp finely grated orange peel
1/8 tsp black pepper
1/4 cup orange juice
1 Tbsp lemon juice

1 Preheat the oven to 400°F. Arrange the halibut in a nonstick baking dish and set aside.

2 Lightly spray a small skillet with nonstick cooking spray. Sauté the onions and garlic for 5 minutes. Remove from heat and add remaining ingredients. Stir to mix and pour over fish.

3 Cover the baking dish with foil and bake for 10–15 minutes or until the halibut flakes easily with a fork.

Baked Mustard Cod

Serves 4

Serving size: 1 fillet

Preparation time: 5 minutes

Exchanges
3 Very Lean Meat

Calories 117
   Calories from Fat 8
Total Fat . . . . 1 g
   Saturated Fat. . . . . 0 g
Cholesterol. . . . . 50 mg
Sodium . . . . 278 mg
Carbohydrate. . . . . 4 g
   Dietary Fiber . . . . 0 g
   Sugars . . . . 4 g
Protein . . . . 21 g

4 cod fillets (4 oz each)
1 Tbsp Dijon mustard
1 Tbsp coarse mustard
   ("country-style")
1 Tbsp fat-free yogurt
1 Tbsp fat-free mayonnaise
1/2 tsp EQUAL® for Recipes **or**
1 1/2 packets EQUAL® sweetener **or**
1 Tbsp EQUAL® Spoonful™

1 Heat the oven to 400°F. Place the fish on a nonstick baking sheet.

2 Combine the remaining ingredients in a small bowl and spread on the fish. Bake for 20 minutes.

3 Lay a sheet of foil over the fish, turn oven off, and let fish stand for 5 minutes before serving.

Crab Cakes with Yogurt Tartar Sauce

Serves 4

Serving size: 4 crab cakes

Preparation time: 15 minutes

Exchanges
1/2 Starch
2 Very Lean Meat
1/2 Fat

Calories............. 132
  Calories from Fat 33
Total Fat .... 4 g
  Saturated Fat.......... 1 g
Cholesterol............ 50 mg
Sodium .... 478 mg
Carbohydrate.......... 10 g
  Dietary Fiber.......... 1 g
  Sugars .... 4 g
Protein .... 15 g

1/2 cup fat-free plain yogurt
  1 Tbsp reduced-calorie mayonnaise
  1 Tbsp minced fresh dill
  2 cloves garlic, minced
  1 tsp onion powder
  1 tsp lime juice
1/4 cup egg substitute
  1 Tbsp Dijon mustard
  1 Tbsp fat-free plain yogurt
  2 tsp lite soy sauce
1/4 tsp hot pepper sauce
  8 oz crabmeat, cooked, cartilage removed
1/3 cup finely chopped celery
1/4 cup finely chopped green onions
1/4 cup fine dry breadcrumbs
  1 tsp olive oil

1 In a small bowl, stir together the first 6 ingredients and set the sauce aside.

2 In a medium bowl, combine the remaining ingredients except the olive oil and mix thoroughly.

3 Form the crab mixture into 16 patties. Heat 1/2 tsp oil in a large nonstick skillet over medium heat. Cook 8 crab cakes for 3 minutes on one side, then turn and cook for 3 more minutes or until golden brown.

4 Heat the remaining oil in the skillet and cook the rest of the crab cakes. Serve with the sauce.

Grilled Fish with Pineapple-Cilantro Sauce

Serves 6

Serving size: 1 halibut steak

Preparation time: 15 minutes

Exchanges
1 Fruit
3 Very Lean Meat
1/2 Fat

Calories	190
Calories from Fat	26
Total Fat	3 g
Saturated Fat	0 g
Cholesterol	36 mg
Sodium	69 mg
Carbohydrate	17 g
Dietary Fiber	1 g
Sugars	14 g
Protein	24 g

1 medium pineapple, peeled, cored, and cut into small chunks
3/4 cup unsweetened pineapple juice
2 Tbsp lime juice
2 cloves garlic, minced
1 tsp minced jalapeño pepper
2 Tbsp minced cilantro
2 Tbsp cold water
1 Tbsp cornstarch
1 tsp EQUAL® for Recipes **or**
3 packets EQUAL® sweetener **or**
2 Tbsp EQUAL® Spoonful™
6 4-oz halibut steaks, grilled

1 Heat the pineapple, pineapple juice, lime juice, garlic, and jalapeño pepper to boiling in a medium saucepan. Reduce the heat and simmer, uncovered, for 5 minutes.

2 Stir in the cilantro and heat to boiling. Mix the cold water and cornstarch together; stir into the boiling mixture. Boil, stirring constantly, until thickened.

3 Remove from heat and cool 2–3 minutes. Stir in the Equal® and serve over the fish.

Lemon-Mustard Salmon

Serves 4

Serving size: 1 salmon steak

Preparation time: 10 minutes

Exchanges
4 Lean Meat
1 1/2 Fat

Calories. 284
   Calories from Fat 162
Total Fat . . . . 18 g
   Saturated Fat. . . . . 5 g
Cholesterol. . . . . 78 mg
Sodium . . . . 511 mg
Carbohydrate. . . . . 4 g
   Dietary Fiber . . . . 0 g
   Sugars . . . . 3 g
Protein . . . . 26 g

    4 salmon steaks (4 oz each)
1/4 cup Dijon mustard
1/4 cup coarse mustard
     ("country-style")
1/4 cup white wine vinegar
1/4 cup olive oil
1 1/4 tsp EQUAL® for Recipes **or**
    4 packets EQUAL® sweetener **or**
2 1/2 Tbsp EQUAL® Spoonful™
    2 Tbsp lemon juice
1/2 onion, minced
    2 tsp minced garlic
1/8 tsp black pepper

1 Combine all ingredients except the salmon in a shallow dish. Place the salmon in the dish, cover, and marinate in the refrigerator for 2 hours.

2 Heat oven to broil. Remove the salmon from the marinade and broil (or grill) the salmon for 5–7 minutes on each side or until it flakes easily with a fork.

Oven-Fried Fish

Serves 4

Serving size: 1 fillet

Preparation time: 15 minutes

Exchanges
1 Starch
3 Very Lean Meat
1/2 Fat

Calories. 203
  Calories from Fat 62
Total Fat . . . . 7 g
  Saturated Fat. . . . . 1 g
Cholesterol. . . . . 50 mg
Sodium . . . . 234 mg
Carbohydrate. . . . . 11 g
  Dietary Fiber. . . . . 1 g
  Sugars . . . . 1 g
Protein . . . . 23 g

3 Tbsp dried breadcrumbs
3 Tbsp cashew flour
   or ground cashews
1/2 tsp basil
1/4 tsp oregano
1/8 tsp garlic powder
3 Tbsp cornmeal
1/4 tsp celery salt
1/8 tsp cayenne pepper
1 Tbsp olive oil
1 slightly beaten egg white
4 4-oz cod fillets

1 Preheat the oven to 450°F. Combine the dry ingredients in a shallow dish. Mix the oil and egg white together and brush over each fillet.

2 Dip each fillet in the breadcrumb mixture and place in nonstick baking dish. Bake uncovered for 15 minutes or until the fish flakes easily with a fork.

Salmon Loaves with Yogurt Dill Sauce

Serves 4

Serving size: 1 loaf

Preparation time: 10 minutes

Exchanges
1/2 Carbohydrate
3 Lean Meat

Calories 187
   Calories from Fat 50
Total Fat . . . . 6 g
   Saturated Fat. . . . . 0 g
Cholesterol. . . . . 49 mg
Sodium . . . . 678 mg
Carbohydrate. . . . . 10 g
   Dietary Fiber . . . . 1 g
   Sugars . . . . 7 g
Protein . . . . 23 g

2 slightly beaten egg whites
1 cup soft breadcrumbs
1/2 cup finely chopped yellow onion
2 Tbsp fat-free milk
1/2 tsp dill
1/8 tsp pepper
2 7 1/2-oz cans salmon, drained, flaked, skin and bones removed
1 cup plain fat-free yogurt
1 Tbsp dill
1 Tbsp Dijon mustard
1 tsp lemon juice
1/2 tsp hot pepper sauce
1/2 tsp onion powder

1 Preheat the oven to 350°F. In a large mixing bowl, stir together the egg whites, breadcrumbs, onion, milk, and 1/2 tsp dill. Stir in the salmon. Divide the mixture into 4 evenly-shaped loaves.

2 Place the loaves in a nonstick baking dish and bake, uncovered, for 20–25 minutes or until lightly browned. Meanwhile, combine the remaining ingredients in a small bowl and drizzle sauce over salmon to serve.

Shrimp Creole

Serves 4

Serving size: 1 cup

Preparation time: 20 minutes

Exchanges
4 Starch
2 Very Lean Meat

Calories 391
   Calories from Fat 64
Total Fat . . . . 7 g
   Saturated Fat . . . . 1 g
Cholesterol . . . . 161 mg
Sodium . . . . 607 mg
Carbohydrate . . . . 57 g
   Dietary Fiber . . . . 2 g
   Sugars . . . . 6 g
Protein . . . . 23 g

2 Tbsp margarine
1 green bell pepper, diced
2 ribs celery, thinly sliced
1 onion, chopped
1/2 tsp oregano
2 cloves garlic, minced
1/8 tsp cayenne pepper
1 1/2 cups tomato juice
1 Tbsp cornstarch
16 large shrimp, shelled
   and deveined
4 cups hot cooked rice
2 Tbsp chopped parsley

1 Melt the margarine over medium heat in a large skillet. Sauté the bell pepper, celery, onion, oregano, garlic, and pepper for 5 minutes. Add 1 cup tomato juice. Heat to boiling.

2 Reduce heat to low, cover, and cook 5 minutes, stirring occasionally. Meanwhile, in a small bowl, stir together the cornstarch and remaining 1/2 cup tomato juice until smooth.

3 Increase heat to medium. Add the cornstarch mixture and shrimp to the vegetable mixture. Cook until the mixture boils and thickens and shrimp turn pink and opaque, stirring constantly. Serve over rice and sprinkle with parsley.

★ *Beef, Pork, & Lamb*

Beef & Pasta

Serves 4

Serving size: 1/4 recipe

Preparation time: 10 minutes

Exchanges
2 Starch
2 Lean Meat
1/2 Fat

Calories. 287
   Calories from Fat 101
Total Fat . . . . 11 g
   Saturated Fat. . . . . 4 g
Cholesterol. . . . . 53 mg
Sodium . . . . 654 mg
Carbohydrate . . . . 27 g
   Dietary Fiber. . . . . 1 g
   Sugars . . . . 4 g
Protein . . . . 20 g

3/4 lb lean ground beef (85% lean)
1 can vegetable broth
1 Tbsp Worcestershire sauce
1/2 tsp oregano
1/2 tsp garlic powder
1 8-oz can stewed tomatoes
1 1/2 cups uncooked shaped pasta

1 Brown the beef over medium-high heat. Add remaining ingredients except pasta and heat to a boil. Add the pasta, reduce heat to low, cover, and cook for 10 minutes, stirring often.

2 Uncover and cook for 5 more minutes or until pasta is done and most of the liquid is absorbed. Garnish with Parmesan cheese if desired.

Down-Home Pulled Pork BBQ

Serves 6

Serving size: 1 sandwich

Preparation time: 20 minutes

Exchanges
2 Starch
2 1/2 Lean Meat

Calories.............352
   Calories from Fat 70
Total Fat ....8 g
   Saturated Fat ......2 1/2 g
Cholesterol..........100 mg
Sodium ....460 mg
Carbohydrate ....28 g
   Dietary Fiber..........3 g
   Sugars ....6 g
Protein ....39 g

1 lb whole pork tenderloin, fat trimmed
1 tsp chili powder
1/2 tsp garlic powder
1/2 cup finely chopped onion
1 1/2 tsp minced garlic
1 15-oz can crushed tomatoes, undrained
1 Tbsp cider vinegar
1 Tbsp prepared mustard
1/4 tsp maple extract
1/4 tsp liquid smoke
1–2 tsp chili powder
2 1/2 tsp EQUAL® for Recipes or
8 packets EQUAL® sweetener or
1/3 cup EQUAL® Spoonful™
Salt and pepper to taste
6 multigrain hamburger buns, toasted

1 Heat oven to 425°F. Rub pork with chili and garlic powders; place in baking pan. Bake until pork is well browned and juices run clear, 30–40 minutes. Let stand 10–15 minutes.

2 Cut slices 2–3 inches thick; shred slices into bite-size pieces with a fork. Spray medium saucepan with nonstick cooking spray; heat over medium heat until hot. Sauté onion and garlic until tender, about 5 minutes.

3 Add tomatoes, vinegar, mustard, maple extract, liquid smoke, and chili powder to saucepan; heat to boiling. Reduce heat and simmer, uncovered, until the sauce is of medium consistency, 10–15 minutes.

4 Stir in Equal®. Season to taste with salt and pepper. Stir pork into sauce; cook until hot, 2–3 minutes. Spoon mixture into buns.

Herbed Lamb Chops

Serves 4

Serving size: 1 chop

Preparation time: 10 minutes

Exchanges
3 Lean Meat

Calories. 143
   Calories from Fat 68
Total Fat . . . . 8 g
   Saturated Fat. . . . . 3 g
Cholesterol. . . . . 56 mg
Sodium . . . . 169 mg
Carbohydrate. . . . . 1 g
   Dietary Fiber . . . . 0 g
   Sugars . . . . 1 g
Protein. . . . . 17 g

4 5-oz lamb chops
1 Tbsp Worcestershire sauce
1 orange, sliced in half
1 tsp Italian seasoning
1/8 tsp black pepper
1/4 tsp seasoning salt
1 tsp olive oil
1 tsp butter

1 Squeeze orange juice into a shallow dish. Add the Worcestershire sauce and stir. Add the lamb chops and marinate covered in the refrigerator for 30 minutes to 2 hours.

2 Remove the lamb chops to a plate and sprinkle with seasonings. In a large skillet, heat the oil over medium-high heat, then add the butter and heat until melted. Add the lamb chops and cook on each side about 4 minutes.

Italian Pepper Steak

Serves 4

Serving size: 1/4 recipe

Preparation time: 15 minutes

Exchanges
4 Starch
3 Lean Meat
1/2 Fat

Calories. 504
   Calories from Fat 122
Total Fat . . . . 14 g
   Saturated Fat. . . . . 3 g
Cholesterol. . . . . 71 mg
Sodium . . . . 569 mg
Carbohydrate. . . . . 61 g
   Dietary Fiber. . . . . 5 g
   Sugars . . . . 15 g
Protein . . . . 33 g

1 lb boneless beef sirloin, sliced into strips
2 Tbsp olive oil
2 cups bell pepper strips (mix green, red, and yellow)
1 medium onion, sliced and separated into rings
1 tsp oregano
2 cloves garlic, minced
1/4 tsp pepper
1 11-oz can condensed tomato soup
1/2 cup water
4 cups hot, cooked pasta

1 Heat the oil in a large skillet over medium-high heat. Sauté all ingredients except the soup, water, and pasta for 10 minutes or until the beef is done.

2 Stir in the soup and water and heat to boiling. Serve over hot pasta.

Marinated Beef Kabobs

Serves 4

Serving size: 2 kabobs

Preparation time: 15 minutes

Exchanges
2 Lean Meat
2 Vegetable

Calories 167
   Calories from Fat 38
Total Fat . . . . 4 g
   Saturated Fat . . . . 1 g
Cholesterol . . . . 48 mg
Sodium . . . . 563 mg
Carbohydrate . . . . 12 g
   Dietary Fiber . . . . 3 g
   Sugars . . . . 8 g
Protein . . . . , . . 20 g

1/3 cup fat-free Italian dressing
1/2 cup dry red wine
    (or vegetable broth)
1 1/2 Tbsp lite soy sauce
  12 oz lean boneless sirloin steak, cut into 1-inch cubes, trimmed of fat
   2 medium zucchini, each cut into 4 pieces
   1 red onion, cut into 8 pieces
   8 large mushrooms
   8 cherry tomatoes
1/2 tsp seasoning salt
1/8 tsp black pepper

1 Combine the Italian dressing, wine, and soy sauce in a shallow bowl. Place the steak pieces in the marinade and marinate covered in the refrigerator for at least 60 minutes (several hours if possible).

2 Heat the oven to broil. Steam the zucchini and onion for 2–3 minutes or until slightly softened but still crisp. Assemble 8 kabobs, alternating meat and vegetables, using 3–4 pieces of meat, 2 zucchini chunks, 2 onion pieces, 2 mushrooms, and 2 tomatoes per skewer.

3 Broil on top oven rack (or grill 5 inches from medium-hot coals) for about 10 minutes or until desired doneness.

Mom's Meatloaf

Serves 8

Serving size: 1 slice

Preparation time: 10 minutes

Exchanges
1 1/2 Starch
3 Lean Meat
1 Vegetable
1 Fat

Calories. 342
   Calories from Fat 133
Total Fat . . . . 15 g
   Saturated Fat. . . . . 6 g
Cholesterol. . . . . 98 mg
Sodium . . . . 440 mg
Carbohydrate . . . . 25 g
   Dietary Fiber. . . . . 3 g
   Sugars . . . . 4 g
Protein . . . . 26 g

2 lb lean ground beef
  (less than 15% fat)
1 egg and 2 egg whites
1 medium onion, diced
1/2 cup Italian breadcrumbs
1 tsp Italian seasoning
3/4 tsp salt
1/2 tsp garlic powder
1/8 tsp pepper
1 lb carrots, peeled and cut in
  large chunks
4 5-oz potatoes, peeled and cut
  in large chunks

1 Heat the oven to 350°F. Combine all ingredients except potatoes and carrots in a large bowl and form into a loaf.

2 Place the loaf on a rack in a roasting pan. Put the carrot and potatoes in the pan and bake for 1 1/4 hours.

Pork Chops with Noodles

Serves 6

Serving size: 1 chop

Preparation time: 15 minutes

Exchanges
3 Starch
3 Lean Meat

Calories. 385
   Calories from Fat 85
Total Fat . . . . 9 g
   Saturated Fat. . . . . 3 g
Cholesterol. . . . . 111 mg
Sodium . . . . 285 mg
Carbohydrate . . . . 44 g
   Dietary Fiber . . . . 2 g
   Sugars . . . . 3 g
Protein . . . . 29 g

2 Tbsp cornstarch
1 can beef broth
1/8 tsp pepper
6 6-oz pork chops (1/2 inch thick)
1 onion, sliced
6 cups hot, cooked egg noodles

1 Mix the cornstarch, broth, and pepper in a bowl until smooth. Set aside. Brown the pork chops in a large skillet on both sides, about 5 minutes each side. Add onion during last 5 minutes.

2 Add the broth and cook until mixture boils and thickens, stirring constantly. Reduce heat to low, cover, and cook 5 minutes or until chops are no longer pink. Serve hot over noodles.

Pork Fajitas with Spicy Apple Salsa

Serves 4

Serving size: 2 fajitas

Preparation time: 20 minutes

Exchanges
3 Starch
3 Lean Meat

Calories 392
   Calories from Fat 84
Total Fat . . . . 9 g
   Saturated Fat . . . . 3 g
Cholesterol . . . . 65 mg
Sodium . . . . 544 mg
Carbohydrate . . . . 47 g
   Dietary Fiber . . . . 6 g
   Sugars . . . . 7 g
Protein . . . . 30 g

4 dried cascabel chiles
1 cup water
2 Tbsp fresh lime juice
1/4 tsp salt
3 large garlic cloves, peeled
1 1-lb pork tenderloin
8 6-inch wheat tortillas
1 cup Spicy Apple Salsa
  (see recipe, page 67)

1 Remove the stems and seeds from the chiles. Combine the chiles and water in a small saucepan and bring to a boil. Remove from heat. Cover and let stand 1 hour.

2 Drain the chiles, reserving 2 Tbsp of soaking liquid. Combine the chiles, reserved soaking liquid, lime juice, salt, and garlic in a blender. Blend until smooth. Trim fat from pork and place pork in a shallow dish. Pour the chile mixture over the pork, cover, and refrigerate for 1 1/2 hours.

3 Preheat the oven to 375 degrees F. Remove the pork from the marinade and bake in a nonstick baking pan for 35 minutes. Wrap the tortillas tightly in foil. Bake in oven for 5 minutes.

4 Remove the pork and tortillas from the oven. Cut the pork diagonally across the grain into thin slices. Stuff the tortillas evenly with the pork slices. Place 2 Tbsp Apple Salsa in the center of each tortilla. Roll up and serve.

Smothered Pork Chops

Serves 6

Serving size: 1 chop

Preparation time: 10 minutes

Exchanges
3 Lean Meat

Calories. 143
   Calories from Fat 68
Total Fat . . . . 8 g
   Saturated Fat. . . . . 3 g
Cholesterol. . . . . 56 mg
Sodium . . . . 169 mg
Carbohydrate. . . . . 1 g
   Dietary Fiber . . . . 0 g
   Sugars . . . . 1 g
Protein. . . . . 17 g

4 5-oz pork chops
1 Tbsp Worcestershire sauce
1 orange, sliced in half
1 tsp Italian seasoning
1/8 tsp black pepper
1/4 tsp seasoning salt
1 tsp olive oil
1 tsp butter

1 Squeeze orange juice into a shallow dish. Add the Worcestershire sauce and stir. Add the pork chops and marinate covered in the refrigerator for 30 minutes to 2 hours.

2 Remove the pork chops to a plate and sprinkle with seasonings. In a large skillet, heat the oil over medium-high heat, then add the butter and heat until melted. Add the pork chops and cook on each side about 4 minutes.

★ Breakfast, Breads, & Muffins

Albert-At-Sea Omelet

Serves 4

Serving size: 1/4 recipe

Preparation time: 20 minutes

Exchanges
2 Medium-Fat Meat
1 Vegetable

Calories 175
   Calories from Fat 90
Total Fat . . . . 10 g
   Saturated Fat . . . . 3 g
Cholesterol . . . . 245 mg
Sodium . . . . 336 mg
Carbohydrate . . . . 3 g
   Dietary Fiber . . . . 1 g
   Sugars . . . . 2 g
Protein . . . . 17 g

1 Tbsp olive oil
1/4 red bell pepper, minced
1/4 yellow bell pepper, minced
1/3 cup mushrooms, chopped and minced
1/2 onion, minced
4 eggs
4 egg whites
1/8 tsp salt
1 tsp garlic herb seasoning
1/8 tsp pepper
1/2 cup baby shrimp, cooked
1 slice bacon, cooked crisp, drained well, and crumbled
1/2 cup shredded low-fat cheddar cheese

1 Heat the oil in a large skillet and sauté the peppers, mushrooms, and onions for 5 minutes. Remove the vegetables from the skillet.

2 Beat the eggs and egg whites and add seasonings. Pour the eggs in the skillet and cook over medium heat for 2 minutes, then flip.

3 Place the vegetables, shrimp, bacon, and cheese on the omelet. Fold omelet over and cook for 2 more minutes.

Banana Bran Muffins

Serves 12

Serving size: 1 muffin

Preparation time: 10 minutes

Exchanges
1 Carbohydrate

Calories 83	
Calories from Fat 23	
Total Fat . . . . 3 g	
Saturated Fat . . . . 0 g	
Cholesterol . . . . 0 mg	
Sodium . . . . 107 mg	
Carbohydrate . . . . 15 g	
Dietary Fiber . . . . 2 g	
Sugars . . . . 9 g	
Protein . . . . 2 g	

2/3 cup 100% bran cereal
1/3 cup fat-free milk
  2 large egg whites, lightly beaten
  2 Tbsp canola oil
1/2 cup mashed ripe banana
1/4 cup honey
1/2 cup whole-wheat flour
  1 tsp baking powder
1/4 tsp salt

1 Preheat the oven to 400 degrees F. Combine the bran cereal and milk in a large bowl and let stand for 5 minutes or until softened. Beat in egg whites and oil. Stir in mashed banana and honey.

2 In a separate bowl, combine flour, baking powder, and salt. Add dry ingredients to banana mixture, stirring just until blended.

3 Fill 12 nonstick muffin cups. Bake 15–18 minutes or until golden brown and firm. Remove from muffin cups to cool.

Blueberry Almond Muffins

Serves: 18

Serving size: 1 muffin

Preparation time: 15 minutes

Exchanges
1 1/2 Carbohydrate
1/2 Fat

Calories 120
   Calories from Fat 33
Total Fat . . . . 4 g
   Saturated Fat . . . . 0 g
Cholesterol . . . . 12 mg
Sodium . . . . 139 mg
Carbohydrate . . . . 20 g
   Dietary Fiber . . . . 1 g
   Sugars . . . . 8 g
Protein . . . . 2 g

2 cups all-purpose flour
2/3 cup granulated sugar
1 Tbsp baking powder
1/2 tsp baking soda
1/4 tsp salt
1/4 cup vegetable oil
1 egg
1 cup low-fat (1%) milk
1/2 Tbsp vanilla extract
1/2 Tbsp almond extract
1 cup fresh or frozen blueberries

Streusel Topping (optional;
not included in nutrient analysis)
1/2 cup almonds, finely chopped
1/2 Tbsp sugar
1 Tbsp melted butter
1/2 tsp molasses

1 Preheat oven to 350°F. In a medium bowl, whisk together flour, sugar, baking powder, baking soda, and salt until well blended, about 1 minute. In another bowl, combine oil, egg, milk, vanilla, and almond extract until well blended.

2 Pour liquid mixture into middle of flour mixture and stir until not quite all combined. Add blueberries and gently finish combining. Spoon batter into 18 muffin cups, filling each about 2/3 full.

3 If using topping, combine topping ingredients in a small bowl and sprinkle evenly over muffins. Bake until a toothpick inserted in the center comes out clean, about 15–18 minutes.

Easy Egg Soufflé

Serves 4

Serving size: 1/4 recipe

Preparation time: 10 minutes

Exchanges
2 Medium-Fat Meat

Calories 153
   Calories from Fat 79
Total Fat . . . . 9 g
   Saturated Fat . . . . 4 g
Cholesterol . . . . 230 mg
Sodium . . . . 169 mg
Carbohydrate . . . . 3 g
   Dietary Fiber . . . . 1 g
   Sugars . . . . 2 g
Protein . . . . 15 g

4 eggs
4 egg whites
1/8 tsp salt
1/8 tsp pepper
1 Tbsp butter
1 oz shredded low-fat cheddar
   cheese
1/4 red bell pepper, minced
1/4 yellow bell pepper, minced
1/4 green bell pepper, minced
1/2 cup chopped mushrooms
1/4 cup cooked, chopped chicken

1 Heat the oven to broil. Beat the eggs and whites and add salt and pepper. Melt the butter in a large oven-proof skillet and add the eggs, gently stirring.

2 As the eggs begin to firm, add the remaining ingredients, putting the cheese evenly on top, then place the dish in the oven with the door opened.

3 When the cheese bubbles, remove the eggs and test by slicing, making sure the dish is firm throughout. Allow the dish to cool a bit to assure firmness. Slice and serve. Great warm or at room temperature.

Italian Baked Eggs

Serves 4

Serving size: 1 slice

Preparation time: 15 minutes

Exchanges
2 Medium-Fat Meat
1/2 Fat

Calories	183
Calories from Fat	110
Total Fat	12 g
Saturated Fat	4 g
Cholesterol	221 mg
Sodium	488 mg
Carbohydrate	3 g
Dietary Fiber	0 g
Sugars	2 g
Protein	15 g

1   Tbsp olive oil
1/2   medium onion, minced
4   eggs
3   egg whites
4   slices bacon, cooked crisp and crumbled
1/2   cup shredded low-fat cheese
1   cup fresh or frozen spinach, chopped
1   tsp Italian herb seasoning
1/4   tsp pepper
1/2   tsp seasoning salt

1   Heat the oven to 350°F. Heat the oil in a small skillet and sauté the onion for 3–4 minutes.

2   Beat the eggs and egg whites and stir in all ingredients, including the onion. Pour mixture into a nonstick quiche pan. Bake for 20 minutes. Check with knife to assure the loaf is done throughout.

Oven-Baked French Toast

Serves 8

Serving size: 1/8 recipe

Preparation time: 15 minutes

Exchanges
2 Starch
1 Very Lean Meat
1/2 Fruit
1/2 Fat

Calories 243
    Calories from Fat 56
Total Fat . . . . 6 g
    Saturated Fat . . . . 2 g
Cholesterol . . . . 109 mg
Sodium . . . . 329 mg
Carbohydrate . . . . 36 g
    Dietary Fiber . . . . 2 g
    Sugars . . . . 10 g
Protein . . . . 11 g

1/3 cup raisins
1/2 cup orange juice
1 loaf egg bread, torn into 1-inch pieces
1 1/2 cups plain or vanilla-flavored soy milk
3 eggs, beaten
3 egg whites, beaten
1 tsp vanilla
1 tsp EQUAL® for Recipes **or**
3 packets EQUAL® sweetener **or**
2 Tbsp EQUAL® Spoonful™
1/4 tsp cinnamon

1 Soak raisins in orange juice for 30 minutes to plump them. Place bread in a large bowl. In a medium bowl, whisk together milk, eggs and whites, and vanilla. Pour mixture over bread.

2 Add raisins with the soaking liquid. With a fork, mix until bread is completely coated. Set aside to soak for 30 minutes. (If preparing the night before, cover with plastic and refrigerate.)

3 Heat the oven to 400°F. Coat 8 × 8 baking dish with nonstick cooking spray and set aside. Spread soaked bread in an even layer in the dish. Combine the Equal® and cinnamon in a small bowl, then sprinkle the mixture over the bread.

4 Bake in the oven for 30 minutes or until the bread is brown and crusty on top and sides are still moist. Serve either hot or warm.

Spicy Chicken Omelet

Serves 4

Serving size: 1/4 recipe

Preparation time: 25 minutes

Exchanges
3 Lean Meat
1 Vegetable
1 1/2 Fat

Calories. 252
   Calories from Fat 146
Total Fat . . . . 16 g
   Saturated Fat. . . . . 5 g
Cholesterol. . . . . 233 mg
Sodium . . . . 716 mg
Carbohydrate. . . . . 6 g
   Dietary Fiber . . . . 1 g
   Sugars . . . . 4 g
Protein . . . . 20 g

1/4 cup pineapple juice
8 oz boneless, skinless chicken breast, cut into chunks
4 eggs
8 egg whites
1 tsp seasoning salt
1/8 tsp black pepper
2 Tbsp olive oil
1/2 onion, minced
1/4 green bell pepper, minced
1/4 red bell pepper, minced
1/4 cup olives, minced
1/2 tsp barbecue herb mix
1/8 tsp cayenne pepper
1/2 cup shredded low-fat cheddar cheese
1 Tbsp minced parsley

1 Pour the pineapple juice over the chicken chunks, cover, and marinate in the refrigerator for 1 hour. Remove the chicken from the juice.

2 Beat the eggs and whites together and add salt and black pepper. Heat 1 Tbsp oil in a large skillet and sauté the chicken, onions, bell peppers, olives, barbecue seasoning, and cayenne pepper for 5–7 minutes.

3 Remove the chicken and veggies from the skillet and heat 1 Tbsp oil. Add the eggs and cook on one side 2 minutes. Flip the omelet and place the meat and veggies evenly on top. Sprinkle with cheese and fold over, cooking for 2 more minutes. Sprinkle with parsley to serve.

Carrot Muffins

Serves: 12

Serving size: 1 muffin

Preparation time: 20 minutes

Exchanges
2 Starch
1/2 Fat

Calories.............. 180
   Calories from Fat 25
Total Fat .... 3 g
   Saturated Fat .... 1/2 g
Cholesterol........... 18 mg
Sodium .... 265 mg
Carbohydrate .... 35 g
   Dietary Fiber.......... 2 g
   Sugars .... 7 g
Protein .... 4 g

1 1/2 cups all-purpose flour
1/2 cup whole-wheat flour
3 1/2 tsp EQUAL® for Recipes **or**
  18 packets EQUAL® sweetener **or**
3/4 cup EQUAL® Spoonful™
1 Tbsp ground cinnamon
1 tsp baking soda
1 teaspoon baking powder
1/2 tsp salt
1 1/2 cups grated carrots or parsnips
1/2 cup raisins or currents
1 egg
2 egg whites
3/4 cup fruit purée fat replacement
  (such as Sunsweet® Lighter
  Bake™) or apple butter
2 Tbsp vegetable oil
1 Tbsp vanilla extract
2 Tbsp finely chopped pecans or
  walnuts (optional)

1 Preheat oven to 375°F. Lightly grease 12 muffin cups or coat with nonstick cooking spray. Whisk flours, Equal®, cinnamon, baking soda, baking powder, and salt in a large bowl. Stir in carrots and raisins.

2 Whisk egg, egg whites, fruit purée, oil, and vanilla in a small bowl. Stir into dry ingredients until just moistened.

3 Spoon batter into muffin cups; sprinkle tops with nuts, if using. Bake for about 20 minutes or until tops spring back when lightly pressed.

★ *Desserts*

Apple Crisp

Serves 8

Serving size: 1/8 recipe

Preparation time: 20 minutes

Exchanges
2 Carbohydrate
1 1/2 Fat

Calories. 196
   Calories from Fat 74
Total Fat . . . . .8 g
   Saturated Fat. . . . . .5 g
Cholesterol. . . . . .20 mg
Sodium . . . . .83 mg
Carbohydrate . . . . .30 g
   Dietary Fiber. . . . . .2 g
   Sugars . . . . .21 g
Protein . . . . .2 g

4 cups apples, peeled and sliced
1/2 cup brown sugar
1/2 cup whole-wheat flour
1/2 cup quick-cooking dry oatmeal
1 tsp cinnamon
1/4 tsp nutmeg
1/3 cup butter, softened

1 Heat the oven to 350°F. Place the apples in an 8 × 8 nonstick baking dish. In a small bowl, blend the rest of the ingredients until crumbly.

2 Spread the topping over the apples. Bake for 30 minutes or until the top is golden and the apples are tender.

Apple Pie

31% calorie reduction from traditional recipe

Serves: 8
Serving size: 1 piece

Preparation time: 20 minutes

Exchanges
1 1/2 Starch
2 Fat
1 Fruit

Calories.............246
   Calories from Fat 90
Total Fat ....10 g
   Saturated Fat..........4 g
Cholesterol...........10 mg
Sodium ....193 mg
Carbohydrate ....40 g
   Dietary Fiber..........2 g
   Sugars ....14 g
Protein ....2 g

    Pastry for double-crust 9-inch pie
3 Tbsp cornstarch
7 1/4 tsp EQUAL® for Recipes **or**
  24 packets EQUAL® sweetener **or**
   1 cup EQUAL® Spoonful™
3/4 tsp ground cinnamon
1/4 tsp ground nutmeg
1/4 tsp salt
   8 cups peeled, cored, and sliced Granny Smith or other baking apples (about 8 medium)

1 Heat oven to 425°F. Roll half the pastry dough on floured surface into a circle 1 inch larger than the inverted pie pan. Ease pastry into pan.

2 Combine cornstarch, Equal®, cinnamon, nutmeg, and salt; sprinkle over apples in large bowl and toss. Arrange apples in pie crust.

3 Roll remaining pastry into circle large enough to fit top of pie. If desired, cut hearts in pastry with cutters; place pastry on pie, seal edges, trim, and flute. Press pastry hearts on pastry.

4 Bake until pastry is golden and apples are tender, 40–50 minutes. Cool on wire rack.

Baked Vanilla Custard

51% calorie reduction from traditional recipe

Serves: 10
Serving size: 1/2 cup

Preparation time: 10 minutes

Exchanges
1/2 Milk
1/2 Lean Meat

Calories. 89
   Calories from Fat 28
Total Fat . . . . .3 g
   Saturated Fat. . . . . .1 g
Cholesterol. . . . . 129 mg
Sodium . . . . 146 mg
Carbohydrate. . . . . .8 g
   Dietary Fiber . . . . .0 g
   Sugars . . . . .7 g
Protein . . . . .7 g

  4 cups fat-free milk
  6 eggs
6 1/4 tsp EQUAL® for Recipes **or**
  21 packets EQUAL® sweetener **or**
3/4 cup plus 2 Tbsp EQUAL®
    Spoonful™
  2 tsp vanilla
1/4 tsp salt
    Ground nutmeg

1 Heat milk just to boiling in a medium saucepan. Let cool 5 minutes. Beat remaining ingredients except nutmeg in a large bowl until smooth. Gradually beat in hot milk.

2 Pour the mixture into 10 custard cups or a 1 1/2-qt glass casserole dish. Sprinkle generously with nutmeg. Place cups or dish in a roasting pan and add 1 inch hot water.

3 Bake uncovered for 45–60 minutes or until a knife inserted in the center comes out clean. Remove cups or dish from roasting pan and cool on wire rack. Chill before serving.

Cinnamon Bread Pudding

34% calorie reduction from traditional recipe

Serves: 6
Serving size: 1/6 recipe

Preparation time: 20 minutes

Exchanges
1 Starch
2 Fat
1/2 Milk

Calories. 202
   Calories from Fat 90
Total Fat . . . . 10 g
   Saturated Fat. . . . . 2 g
Cholesterol. . . . . 37 mg
Sodium . . . . 422 mg
Carbohydrate. . . . . 21 g
   Dietary Fiber . . . . 1 g
   Sugars . . . . 6 g
Protein . . . . 8 g

2 cups fat-free milk
4 Tbsp margarine, cut into pieces
1 egg
2 egg whites
5 tsp EQUAL® for Recipes **or**
16 packets EQUAL® sweetener **or**
2/3 cup EQUAL® Spoonful™
1 1/2 tsp ground cinnamon
1/8 tsp ground cloves
3 dashes ground mace (optional)
1/4 tsp salt
4 cups cubed day-old French or Italian bread (3/4-inch-thick slices)

1 Heat the oven to 350°F. Heat milk and margarine to simmering in medium saucepan; remove from heat and stir until margarine is melted. Cool 10 minutes.

2 Beat egg and egg whites in large bowl until foamy; mix in Equal®, spices, and salt. Mix milk mixture into egg mixture; mix in bread. Spoon mixture into ungreased 1 1/2-qt casserole.

3 Place casserole in roasting pan on oven rack; add 1 inch hot water. Bake, uncovered, until pudding is set and sharp knife inserted halfway between center and edge comes out clean, 40–45 minutes.

Chocolate Almond Mousse

Serves 6

Serving size: 1/2 cup

Preparation time: 5 minutes

Exchanges
1 Carbohydrate
1/2 Fat

Calories. 92	
Calories from Fat 22	
Total Fat . . . . 2 g	
Saturated Fat. . . . . 2 g	
Cholesterol. . . . . 2 mg	
Sodium . . . . 135 mg	
Carbohydrate. . . . . 14 g	
Dietary Fiber . . . . 1 g	
Sugars . . . . 9 g	
Protein . . . . 4 g	

1 pkg instant sugar-free chocolate pudding
2 cups fat-free, lactose-free milk
1/8 tsp almond extract
1/8 tsp vanilla
1 envelope whipped topping mix (prepare with fat-free, lactose-free milk)
Cocoa powder for garnish

1 Prepare the chocolate pudding as directed, adding the almond and vanilla extracts to the milk. Prepare the whipped topping as directed.

2 Fold 1 2/3 cups of the whipped topping into the pudding, reserving the remainder of the whipped topping. Spoon into 6 serving goblets and chill for several hours until firm.

3 Garnish with the remaining whipped cream and a sprinkle of cocoa powder. Serve chilled.

Cranberry Apple Crisp

59% calorie reduction from traditional recipe

Serves: 8
Serving size: 1/8 recipe

Preparation time: 20 minutes

Exchanges
1 Fruit
1 1/2 Fat

Calories	145
Calories from Fat	80
Total Fat	8 g
Saturated Fat	1 1/2 g
Cholesterol	0 mg
Sodium	67 mg
Carbohydrate	18 g
Dietary Fiber	2 g
Sugars	7 g
Protein	1 g

3 cups apples, peeled and sliced
2 cups fresh cranberries
7 1/4 tsp EQUAL® for Recipes **or**
24 packets EQUAL® sweetener **or**
1 cup EQUAL® Spoonful™
1/3 cup all-purpose flour
1/4 cup chopped pecans
1/4 cup margarine, melted
3 1/2 tsp EQUAL® for Recipes **or**
12 packets EQUAL® sweetener **or**
1/2 cup EQUAL® Spoonful™

1 Heat the oven to 350°F. Combine apples, cranberries, and 7 1/4 tsp Equal® for Recipes in an ungreased 10-inch glass pie plate.

2 In a separate bowl, mix together flour, pecans, margarine, and 3 1/2 tsp Equal® for Recipes. Sprinkle mixture over top of the apples and cranberries.

3 Bake approximately 1 hour or until bubbly and lightly browned. Delicious served as an accompaniment to pork or poultry or with frozen yogurt as a dessert.

Creamy Rice Pudding

49% calorie reduction from traditional recipe

Serves: 6
Serving size: 2/3 cup

Preparation time: 20 minutes

Exchanges
2 Starch
1/2 Fat
1 Milk

Calories. 244
   Calories from Fat 30
Total Fat . . . . 3 g
   Saturated Fat. . . . . 1 g
Cholesterol. . . . . 109 mg
Sodium . . . . 200 mg
Carbohydrate . . . . 43 g
   Dietary Fiber. . . . . 1 g
   Sugars . . . . 14 g
Protein . . . . 11 g

  2 cups water
  1 cinnamon stick, broken into pieces
  1 cup converted rice
  4 cups fat-free milk
1/4 tsp salt
7 1/4 tsp EQUAL® for Recipes **or**
 24 packets EQUAL® sweetener **or**
  1 cup EQUAL® Spoonful™
  3 egg yolks
  2 egg whites
  1 tsp vanilla
1/4 cup raisins
    Ground cinnamon
    Ground nutmeg

1 Heat water and cinnamon stick to boiling in large saucepan; stir in rice. Reduce heat and simmer, covered, until rice is tender and water absorbed, 20–25 minutes. Discard cinnamon stick.

2 Add milk and salt; heat to boiling. Reduce heat and simmer, covered, until mixture starts to thicken, about 15–20 minutes, stirring frequently. Milk will not be absorbed and pudding will thicken when it cools. Remove from heat and cool 1–2 minutes; stir in Equal®.

3 Beat egg yolks, egg whites, and vanilla in small bowl. Stir about 1/2 cup rice mixture into egg mixture; stir back in saucepan. Cook over low heat, stirring constantly, 1–2 minutes. Stir in raisins.

4 Spoon pudding into serving bowl and sprinkle with cinnamon and nutmeg. Serve warm or room temperature.

Crunchy Critter Mix

Serves 16

Serving size: 1/2 cup

Preparation time: 5 minutes

Exchanges
1 Starch
1/2 Fat

Calories. 90
   Calories from Fat 29
Total Fat . . . . 3 g
   Saturated Fat. . . . . 2 g
Cholesterol. . . . . 6 mg
Sodium . . . . 156 mg
Carbohydrate. . . . . 14 g
   Dietary Fiber . . . . 1 g
   Sugars . . . . 3 g
Protein . . . . 1 g

1 tsp EQUAL® for Recipes **or**
2 packets EQUAL® sweetener **or**
1 1/2 Tbsp EQUAL® Spoonful™
1/4 tsp molasses
3 Tbsp butter
1 tsp cinnamon
1 1/2 cups animal crackers
1 1/2 cups graham cracker bears
1 1/2 cups corn or rice cereal squares
1 1/2 cups oat O's cereal
1 cup tiny unsalted pretzels
1 cup mini whole-wheat cereal squares

1 Heat the oven to 350°F. Combine the Equal®, molasses, and butter in a small bowl. Microwave until the butter melts and the Equal is dissolved. Stir in the cinnamon.

2 Combine the remaining ingredients and mix well. Pour the mixture into a nonstick 13 × 9 baking dish and drizzle with the butter mixture. Toss gently to coat.

3 Bake for 20 minutes, stirring occasionally. Cool completely, then store in an airtight container.

Frozen Yogurt Pumpkin Squares

Serves 18

Serving size: 1 square

Preparation time: 15 minutes

Exchanges
2 Carbohydrate

Calories 177
   Calories from Fat 17
Total Fat . . . . 2 g
   Saturated Fat. . . . . 0 g
Cholesterol. . . . . 0 mg
Sodium . . . . 200 mg
Carbohydrate . . . . 35 g
   Dietary Fiber . . . . 1 g
   Sugars . . . . 24 g
Protein . . . . 5 g

  4 dozen gingersnaps, coarsely crushed
  1 15-oz can pumpkin
1 3/4 tsp EQUAL® for Recipes **or**
  6 packets EQUAL® sweetener **or**
1/4 cup EQUAL® Spoonful™
1/2 tsp ginger
1/2 tsp cinnamon
1/4 tsp nutmeg
1/2 gallon fat-free vanilla frozen yogurt, softened

1 Sprinkle one-third of the gingersnap crumbs onto the bottom of a 13 × 9 pan. Combine the remaining ingredients and mix well. Pour half of the pumpkin mixture over the gingersnaps.

2 Repeat, finishing with 1/3 of the gingersnaps on top. Freeze at least 2 hours. To serve, let sit at room temperature for 5 minutes. Cut into 18 squares.

Lemon Squares

50% calorie reduction from traditional recipe

Serves: 16
Serving size: 1 square

Preparation time: 20 minutes

Exchanges
1/2 Starch
1 1/2 Fat

Calories 104
   Calories from Fat 70
Total Fat . . . . .8 g
   Saturated Fat . . . . . . 1 1/2 g
Cholesterol . . . . .27 mg
Sodium . . . . 109 mg
Carbohydrate . . . . .7 g
   Dietary Fiber . . . . .0 g
   Sugars . . . . .0 g
Protein . . . . .1 g

3/4 cup all-purpose flour
2 1/2 tsp EQUAL® for Recipes **or**
   8 packets EQUAL® sweetener **or**
1/3 cup EQUAL® Spoonful'
2 1/4 tsp cornstarch
1/8 tsp salt
   6 Tbsp cold margarine, cut into pieces
3/4 tsp vanilla
   1 tsp lemon rind
   2 eggs
5 1/2 tsp EQUAL® for Recipes **or**
   18 packets EQUAL® sweetener **or**
3/4 cup EQUAL® Spoonful™
1/4 cup plus 2 Tbsp lemon juice
   4 Tbsp margarine, melted and cooled
   1 Tbsp grated lemon rind

1 Heat the oven to 350°F. Combine flour, 2 1/2 tsp EQUAL® for Recipes, cornstarch, and salt in medium bowl; cut in margarine until mixture resembles coarse crumbs. Sprinkle with vanilla and lemon rind; mix with hands to form dough.

2 Press dough evenly on bottom and 1/4 inch up the side of an 8 × 8 baking pan. Bake until lightly browned, about 10 minutes. Cool on wire rack.

3 Beat eggs and 5 1/2 tsp EQUAL® for Recipes; mix in lemon juice, margarine, and lemon rind. Pour mixture into baked pastry. Bake in 350°F oven until lemon filling is set, about 15 minutes. Cool on wire rack.

Mango-Banana Frozen Yogurt

Serves 6

Serving size: 1/2 cup

Preparation time: 10 minutes

Exchanges
2 1/2 Carbohydrate

Calories 173
   Calories from Fat 11
Total Fat . . . . 1 g
   Saturated Fat . . . . 1 g
Cholesterol . . . . 8 mg
Sodium . . . . 78 mg
Carbohydrate . . . . 36 g
   Dietary Fiber . . . . 1 g
   Sugars . . . . 33 g
Protein . . . . 6 g

   1 cup sliced ripe banana
3/4 cup mango, peeled and chopped
1/2 cup orange juice
   3 Tbsp lime juice
1 1/2 cups fat-free, lactose-free milk
1 3/4 tsp EQUAL® for Recipes **or**
   6 packets EQUAL® sweetener **or**
1/4 cup EQUAL® Spoonful™
   1 16-oz carton low-fat vanilla yogurt

1 Place the banana, mango, orange juice, and lime juice in a blender or food processor and blend until smooth. Add the remaining ingredients and blend for 30 seconds or until smooth.

2 Freeze in individual serving dishes or a freezer-safe container.

Oatmeal Mounds

Serves 20

Serving size: 2 cookies

Preparation time: 15 minutes

Exchanges
1/2 Carbohydrate
1 Fat

Calories	88
Calories from Fat	45
Total Fat	5 g
Saturated Fat	3 g
Cholesterol	12 mg
Sodium	16 mg
Carbohydrate	10 g
Dietary Fiber	1 g
Sugars	4 g
Protein	1 g

1 1/2 cups quick-cooking dry oats
1/4 cup all-purpose flour
1/4 cup whole-wheat flour
1/4 cup firmly packed brown sugar
1/2 tsp cinnamon
1/8 tsp salt
1/2 cup unsalted butter, melted
1 Tbsp honey

1 Heat the oven to 375°F. Mix together the oats, flours, brown sugar, cinnamon, and salt in a medium bowl. Add the butter and honey to the dry ingredients. Mix well.

2 Drop dough by teaspoonfuls 2 inches apart on nonstick baking sheets. Bake for 8–10 minutes or until lightly browned. Remove cookies from the oven and let them harden on the baking sheets before transferring to wire racks to cool (approximately 2 minutes).

Raspberry-Almond Bars

34% calorie reduction from traditional recipe

Serves: 24
Serving size: 1 bar

Preparation time: 20 minutes

Exchanges
1 Starch
1 Fat

Calories 116
   Calories from Fat 50
Total Fat . . . . 6 g
   Saturated Fat. . . . . 1 g
Cholesterol. . . . . 9 mg
Sodium . . . . 59 mg
Carbohydrate. . . . . 15 g
   Dietary Fiber. . . . . 0 g
   Sugars . . . . 6 g
Protein . . . . 2 g

  2 cups all-purpose flour
3 1/2 tsp EQUAL® for Recipes **or**
 12 packets EQUAL® sweetener **or**
1/2 cup EQUAL® Spoonful™
1/8 tsp salt
  8 Tbsp cold margarine, cut into pieces
  1 large egg
  1 Tbsp fat-free milk or water
  2 tsp grated lemon peel
2/3 cup seedless raspberry spreadable fruit
  1 tsp cornstarch
1/2 cup sliced toasted almonds (or walnut or pecan pieces)

1 Heat the oven to 400°F. Combine flour, Equal®, and salt in a medium bowl. Cut in margarine with pastry blender until mixture resembles coarse crumbs. Mix in egg, milk, and lemon peel (mixture will be crumbly).

2 Press mixture evenly in bottom of greased 11 × 7 baking dish. Bake until edges of crust are browned, about 15 minutes. Cool on wire rack.

3 Mix spreadable fruit and cornstarch in small saucepan; heat to boiling. Boil until thickened, stirring constantly, 1 minute; cool until warm. Spread mixture evenly over cooled crust; sprinkle with almonds.

4 Bake in 400°F oven until spreadable fruit is thick and bubbly, about 15 minutes. Cool on wire rack. Cut into bars to serve.

Sweet Potato Pie

27% calorie reduction from traditional recipe

Serves: 16 (2 pies)
Serving size: 1 piece

Preparation time: 20 minutes

Exchanges
2 Starch
1 Vegetable
1 1/2 Fat

Calories 212
   Calories from Fat 60
Total Fat . . . . 7 g
   Saturated Fat . . . . . . 2 1/2 g
Cholesterol . . . . 34 mg
Sodium . . . . 260 mg
Carbohydrate . . . . 35 g
   Dietary Fiber . . . . 2 g
   Sugars . . . . 16 g
Protein . . . . 5 g

  3 lb sweet potatoes
2 1/2 cups reduced-fat (2%) milk
  2 eggs, lightly beaten
12 1/2 tsp EQUAL® for Recipes **or**
  42 packets EQUAL® sweetener **or**
1 3/4 cups EQUAL® Spoonful™
1/4 cup cake flour
  1 Tbsp cornstarch
  2 tsp cinnamon
1/2 tsp nutmeg
1/4 tsp ground cloves
3/4 tsp kosher salt
  2 pastries for single crust 9-inch pie

1 Heat oven to 350°F. Bake sweet potatoes until tender (approximately 30–40 minutes); cool slightly, peel, and set aside. Raise oven temperature to 375°F.

2 Simmer milk at medium heat for 5 minutes, reducing the volume to approximately 3/4 cup. Cool slightly.

3 Combine sweet potatoes, eggs, Equal®, and remaining dry ingredients. Beat until smooth while adding the milk slowly. Mix thoroughly.

4 Prick unbaked pie pastries with tines of fork. Pour mixture into 2 pastries. Bake pies for 35 minutes. Cool on wire rack.

New York Cheesecake

39% calorie reduction from traditional recipe

Serves: 16
Serving size: 1 slice

Preparation time: 20 minutes

Exchanges
1 Milk
2 1/2 Fat

Calories 187
   Calories from Fat 110
Total Fat . . . . 12 g
   Saturated Fat. . . . . 6 g
Cholesterol. . . . . 56 mg
Sodium . . . . 253 mg
Carbohydrate. . . . . 13 g
   Dietary Fiber . . . . 0 g
   Sugars . . . . 6 g
Protein . . . . 7 g

1 1/4 cups vanilla wafer crumbs
   4 Tbsp margarine, melted
   1 tsp EQUAL® for Recipes **or**
   3 packets EQUAL® sweetener **or**
   2 Tbsp EQUAL® Spoonful™
  16 oz reduced-fat cream cheese, softened
   8 oz fat-free cream cheese, softened
5 1/2 tsp EQUAL® for Recipes **or**
  18 packets EQUAL® sweetener **or**
 3/4 cup EQUAL® Spoonful™
   2 eggs
   2 eggs whites
   2 Tbsp cornstarch
   1 cup reduced-fat sour cream
   1 tsp vanilla
   1 pint strawberries, sliced (optional)
   1 recipe Strawberry Sauce (optional; see page 188)

1 Heat oven to 350°F. Mix vanilla wafer crumbs, margarine, and 1 tsp EQUAL® for Recipes in the bottom of a 9-inch springform pan. Measure and reserve 1 Tbsp of this crumb mixture.

2 Pat remaining mixture evenly on bottom and 1/2 inch up the side of the pan. Bake until crust is lightly browned, about 8 minutes. Cool on wire rack. Reduce oven temperature to 300°F.

3 Beat cream cheese and 5 1/2 tsp EQUAL® for Recipes in a large bowl until fluffy; beat in eggs, egg whites, and cornstarch. Mix in sour cream and vanilla until well blended. Pour mixture into crust in pan.

4 Place cheesecake in roasting pan on oven rack; add 1 inch hot water to roasting pan. Bake just until set in the center, 45–60 minutes.

5 Remove cheesecake from roasting pan, sprinkle with reserved crumbs, and return to oven. Turn oven off and let cheesecake cool in oven with door ajar for 3 hours. Refrigerate 8 hours or overnight.

6 Remove side of pan; place cheesecake on serving plate. Serve with strawberries and Strawberry Sauce.

Peach Almond Upside-Down

68% calorie reduction from traditional recipe

Serves: 8
Serving size: 1 slice

Preparation time: 20 minutes

Exchanges
1 Starch
1/2 Fruit

Calories 115
   Calories from Fat 20
Total Fat . . . . 2 g
   Saturated Fat. . . . . 0 g
Cholesterol. . . . . 27 mg
Sodium . . . . 193 mg
Carbohydrate . . . . 22 g
   Dietary Fiber . . . . 1 g
   Sugars . . . . 6 g
Protein . . . . 3 g

1 8 1/4-oz can sliced peaches
   packed in water or juice
1/2 cup unsweetened applesauce
5 1/2 tsp EQUAL® for Recipes **or**
  18 packets EQUAL® sweetener **or**
3/4 cup EQUAL® Spoonful™
1 egg
1/2 tsp vanilla
1 cup cake flour
1 tsp baking powder
1/4 tsp baking soda
1/2 tsp ground cinnamon
1/8–1/4 tsp ground nutmeg
1/4 tsp salt
1/2 cup buttermilk

Fruit Topping
3 Tbsp light apricot preserves
   with NutraSweet® brand
   sweetener **or** apricot
   spreadable fruit
1 tsp lemon juice
1 tsp cornstarch
1 3/4 tsp EQUAL® for Recipes **or**
  6 packets EQUAL® sweetener **or**
1/4 cup EQUAL® Spoonful™
1/4 tsp maple extract
1/4 cup sliced almonds, toasted

1 Heat oven to 350°F. Cut peach slices into thirds; arrange in bottom of lightly greased 8-inch cake pan. Mix applesauce, Equal®, egg, and vanilla until smooth in medium bowl.

2 Mix in combined cake flour, baking powder, baking soda, cinnamon, nutmeg, and salt alternately with buttermilk, beginning and ending with dry ingredients. Pour batter over peach slices in pan. Bake until cake is browned and toothpick inserted in center comes out clean, about 20 minutes.

3 While cake is baking, mix preserves, lemon juice, and cornstarch in a small saucepan; heat to boiling, stirring constantly. Remove from heat; stir in Equal and maple extract.

4 When cake is done, invert cake immediately onto serving plate. Spread topping over warm cake and sprinkle with almonds. Serve warm.

Strawberry Sauce

45% calorie reduction from traditional recipe

Serves: 16
Serving size: 2 Tbsp

Preparation time: 5 minutes

Exchanges
Free Food

Calories 12
    Calories from Fat 0
Total Fat . . . . 0 g
    Saturated Fat. . . . . 0 g
Cholesterol. . . . . 0 mg
Sodium . . . . 1 mg
Carbohydrate. . . . . 3 g
    Dietary Fiber . . . . 1 g
    Sugars . . . . 2 g
Protein . . . . 0 g

16 oz frozen unsweetened
    strawberries, thawed
1 Tbsp lemon juice
1 3/4 tsp EQUAL® for Recipes **or**
    6 packets EQUAL® sweetener **or**
1/4 cup EQUAL® Spoonful™

1 Process strawberries in blender or food processor until smooth. Stir in lemon juice and Equal®. Refrigerate until serving time.

Alphabetical List of Recipes

★ *Subject Index*

About the American Diabetes Association

The American Diabetes Association is the nation's leading voluntary health organization supporting diabetes research, information, and advocacy. Its mission is to prevent and cure diabetes and to improve the lives of all people affected by diabetes. The American Diabetes Association is the leading publisher of comprehensive diabetes information. Its huge library of practical and authoritative books for people with diabetes covers every aspect of self-care—cooking and nutrition, fitness, weight control, medications, complications, emotional issues, and general self-care.

To order American Diabetes Association books: Call 1-800-232-6733. http://store.diabetes.org (Note: there is no need to use **www** when typing this particular Web address.)

To join the American Diabetes Association: Call 1-800-806-7801. www.diabetes.org/ membership

For more information about diabetes or ADA programs and services: Call 1-800-342-2383. E-mail: Customerservice@diabetes.org

To locate an ADA/NCQA Recognized Provider of quality diabetes care in your area: Call 1-703-549-1500 ext. 2202. www.diabetes.org/recognition/Physicians/ ListAll.asp

To find an ADA Recognized Education Program in your area: Call 1-888-232-0822. www.diabetes.org/recognition/education.asp

To join the fight to increase funding for diabetes research, end discrimination, and improve insurance coverage: Call 1-800-342-2383. www.diabetes.org/advocacy

To find out how you can get involved with the programs in your community: Call 1-800-342-2383. See below for program Web addresses.

- *American Diabetes Month:* Educational activities aimed at those diagnosed with diabetes—month of November. www.diabetes.org/ADM

- *American Diabetes Alert:* Annual public awareness campaign to find the undiagnosed—held the fourth Tuesday in March. www.diabetes.org/alert

- *The Diabetes Assistance & Resources Program (DAR):* diabetes awareness program targeted to the Latino community. www.diabetes.org/DAR

- *African American Program:* diabetes awareness program targeted to the African American community. www.diabetes.org/africanamerican

- *Awakening the Spirit: Pathways to Diabetes Prevention & Control:* diabetes awareness program targeted to the Native American community. www.diabetes.org/awakening

To find out about an important research project regarding type 2 diabetes: www.diabetes.org/ada/research.asp

To obtain information on making a planned gift or charitable bequest: Call 1-888-700-7029. www.diabetes.org/ada/plan.asp

To make a donation or memorial contribution: Call 1-800-342-2383. www.diabetes.org/ada/cont.asp